From a Raw Deal to a New Deal?

AFRICAN AMERICANS
1929–1945

THE YOUNG OXFORD HISTORY OF
AFRICAN AMERICANS

Robin D. G. Kelley and Earl Lewis
General Editors

From a Raw Deal to a New Deal?

◇ ◇ ◇

AFRICAN AMERICANS
1929–1945

JOE WILLIAM TROTTER, JR.

Oxford University Press
New York • Oxford

Oxford University Press

Oxford   New York
Athens   Auckland   Bangkok   Bombay
Calcutta   Cape Town   Dar es Salaam   Delhi
Florence   Hong Kong   Istanbul   Karachi
Kuala Lumpur   Madras   Madrid   Melbourne
Mexico City   Nairobi   Paris   Singapore
Taipei   Tokyo   Toronto
and associated companies in
Berlin   Ibadan

Published by Oxford University Press, Inc.,
198 Madison Avenue, New York, New York 10016

Library of Congress Cataloging-in Publication Data
Trotter, Joe William
From a raw deal to a new deal? : African Americans, 1929–1945 / Joe William Trotter, Jr.
p.   cm.   — (The Young Oxford history of African Americans ; vol. 8)
Includes bibliographical references and index.
ISBN 0-19-508771-2 (library ed.); ISBN 0-19-508502-7 (series, library ed.)
1. Afro-Americans—History—1877–1964—Juvenile literature.
2. Civil rights movements—United States—History—20th century—Juvenile literature.
3. United States—History—1933–1945—Juvenile literature.
4. United States—History—1919–1933—Juvenile literature.
I. Title. II. Series.
E185.6.T76   1995
973'.0496073—dc20   95-17348
CIP

1 3 5 7 9 8 6 4 2

Printed in the United States of America
on acid-free paper

Design: Sandy Kaufman
Layout: Loraine Machlin
Picture research: Lisa Kirchner, Laura Kreiss

On the cover: Archibald Motley, Jr., *Black Belt,* 1934.
Frontispiece: An evicted sharecropper with his child, New Madrid County, Missouri, 1939.
Page 13: Detail from *The Contribution of the Negro to Democracy in America,* (1943) by Charles White, 11'9" x 17'3"
Hampton University Museum, Hampton, Virginia.

CONTENTS

◇ ◇ ◇

This book is dedicated to young African Americans throughout the diaspora and especially my nieces and nephews:

Salena	Martin
Donald	Charles
Darlene	Rachier
Bruce	Rafiqah
Gregory	Anessah
Terry	Atiyyah
David	Rahmaan
Marva Ann	Raushanah
Geneva (deceased)	Shareefah
Thelma Cassandra	Sherita
Beverly Ann	Sean
Cherelle	Ashley
David Y.	Carson Ray
Joshua	Katie Elizabeth
Moses	Annette Beverly
Margaret Ann	Shenika
Bobbie Jean	Wilena
Isaiah	Malcolm Daniel
Usen	Jamyla Naomi
Rickey, Jr.	

ROBIN D. G. KELLEY
EARL LEWIS

INTRODUCTION

H ard times produce as much humor as despair. In the midst of the Great Depression, African Americans told a popular joke about two black men walking along a country road. Although these men had no money, owned no property, and picked cotton from sunup to sundown, earning barely enough to put food on the table, they took considerable pride in their wives' creative solutions for getting by with so little. Their families endured poverty precisely because these women found ways to turn nothing into something useful. In what must have been an effort to win bragging rights, one of the men announced, "My wife is smart. She don't waste a thing. Why, just the other day she took one of her old raggedy dresses and made me a tie." Not to be outdone, the other fellow turned to his friend and replied, "Boy, that ain't nothing. Yesterday my wife took one of my old ties and made her a dress!"

Thousands of jokes like these circulated throughout African-American communities during the 1930s. Such stories not only provided a light moment in desperate times but also reveal much about the conditions of life and the methods black people adopted to survive one of the most devastating economic crises in the history of the modern world. On the one hand, the fact that one man's wife could *fit* into a tie-sized dress subtly illustrates the desperate straits the black poor were in at the time. On the other hand, the joke speaks volumes to the ways in which African Americans, like many other Americans hurt by the crisis, developed creative ways to cope. In other words, in the worst of times a small glimmer of hope seemed to prevail.

Hope in the midst of crisis is a major theme in the history of the 1930s and '40s. Alongside images of bank closings, endless soup lines,

An employee of the Bethlehem-Fairfield shipyard in Baltimore working on the SS Frederick Douglass *in May 1943. More than 6,000 African Americans were employed at this shipyard during World War II.*

9

jobless men selling apples, unemployed work-ers begging for work, and hard-working middle-class Americans losing everything, we find newsreel footage of families glued to radios listening to the President's inspirational speeches, labor leaders declaring victory in the aftermath of militant strikes, radical pro-testers fighting tenaciously to transform the country. This sense of hope and high expecta-tion was also evident in the many letters ordinary people sent to President Franklin Delano Roosevelt, the man Americans elected President four times in a row beginning in 1932. They believed things would change, that the nation would rise up out of the depression. Roosevelt himself reinforced their hopes by promising a "New Deal" for all Americans. For African Americans in particular, the era

A worker in a Pitts-burgh steel mill, July 1938. Although black workers were the last hired and the first fired, some retained their footing in indus-trial jobs during the Great Depression.

was one of promise and pain: black workers had the highest unemploy-ment rate at a time when black leaders held important positions in Roosevelt's administration; New Deal legislation threw hundreds of thousands of black sharecroppers off the land when the same federal government provided unprecedented opportunities for black writers and artists; dramatic episodes of racist violence against African Americans opened the decade just when Communists and other radicals launched a nationwide campaign against racial injustice.

This sense of hope amid crisis became even more pronounced once the United States entered World War II in 1941. For African Americans, the horrors of war provided an opportunity to demand equal treatment. They criticized the United States for fighting for democracy overseas while black people at home were treated like second-class citizens. Un-like World War I, this time around black leaders called for a "Double Victory"—a victory against fascism abroad and racism at home. The war also created employment opportunities for many black working people, many of whom left the South permanently for the sprawling factories of the urban North. Hopeful that these northern metropolises would be the "promised land," a good number of these migrants found only frustration and disappointment, since only a comparatively small proportion of

A platoon of African-American troops surrounds a farmhouse in France on June 10, 1944. Nearly 1 million black men and women served in the armed forces during World War II.

African Americans gained access to industrial jobs and training programs. Those who did obtain good-paying jobs often experienced violent reprisals from disgruntled white workers who refused to work with blacks. Thus, throughout the war white workers waged "hate strikes" to protest the promotion of blacks, and black workers frequently retaliated with their own strikes to protest discrimination. And, in many instances, racial tensions spread beyond the workplace, erupting in riots in several major U.S. cities. Spurred by poor housing and living conditions in ghettos, competition between blacks and whites over the use of public parks, and police treatment of black citizens, these riots resulted in several deaths, thousands of injuries, and millions of dollars in property damage. Indeed, it might be said that while U.S. troops invaded Normandy and bombed Okinawa, African Americans in the urban ghettos fought their own war at home.

This book explores the various battles waged by African Americans during two of the worst crises the United States had to face in the 20th century. It powerfully demonstrates how each crisis offered a ray of hope, a belief that fighting back can make a difference and that full equality is a basic right. Beginning with the increasingly militant mood of African Americans on the eve of the depression, *From a Raw Deal to a*

New Deal? examines the impact of the economic crisis on black communities, the response on the part of workers, farmers, activists, and the federal government to the depression, the inspiring cultural and intellectual achievements of leading African Americans during the 1930s, and the role that wartime industrialization and recovery played in black protest movements. The book concludes by linking the movements of the 1930s and '40s to the beginnings of the modern civil rights movement.

This book is part of an 11-volume series that narrates African-American history from the 15th through the 20th centuries. Since the 1960s, a rapid explosion in research on black Americans has significantly modified previous understanding of that experience. Studies of slavery, African-American culture, social protest, families, and religion, for example, silenced those who had previously labeled black Americans insignificant historical actors. This new research followed a general upsurge of interest in the social and cultural experiences of the supposedly powerless men and women who did not control the visible reins of power. The result has been a careful and illuminating portrait of how ordinary people make history and serve as the architects of their own destinies.

This series explores many aspects of the lives of African Americans. It describes how blacks shaped and changed the history of this nation. It also places the lives of African Americans in the context of the Americas as a whole. We start the story more than a century before the day in 1619 when 19 "negars" stepped off a Spanish ship in Jamestown, Virginia, and end with the relationship between West Indian immigrants and African Americans in large urban centers like New York in the late 20th century.

At the same time, the series addresses a number of interrelated questions: What was life like for the first Africans to land in the Americas, and what were the implications for future African Americans? Were all Africans and African Americans enslaved? How did race shape slavery and how did slavery influence racism? The series also considers questions about male–female relationships, the forging of African-American communities, religious beliefs and practices, the experiences of the young, and the changing nature of social protest. The key events in American history are here, too, but viewed from the perspective of African Americans. The result is a fascinating and compelling story of nearly five centuries of African-American history.

THE YOUNG OXFORD HISTORY OF
AFRICAN AMERICANS

THE RISE OF THE "NEW NEGRO"

◇ ◇ ◇

Following the end of slavery, most African Americans worked as sharecroppers on southern farms. The novelist Richard Wright, born on a plantation near Natchez, Mississippi, in 1908, later described the dilemma facing African-American sharecroppers in the rural South. "When we grumble about our hard life," he said, "the Lords of the Land cry: 'Listen, I've borrowed money on my plantation and I'm risking my *land* with you folks!' And we, hungry and barefoot, cry: 'And we're risking our *lives* with you!'"

Although some blacks had moved to urban areas following the Civil War, it was only during World War I that blacks moved to cities in large numbers. World War I opened up new opportunities for African Americans in the nation's major industrial centers. For the first time in the nation's history, African Americans broke through the agricultural "job ceiling" and entered the industrial sector in rising numbers. They gained jobs in the iron, steel, automobile, meatpacking, and other mass production industries. An estimated 500,000 blacks left the South for northern and western cities between 1916 and 1920; another 800,000 to 1 million departed during the 1920s. At the same time, African Americans increased their numbers in southern cities. By 1930 an estimated 5.1 million blacks lived in cities, an increase from about 27 percent of all blacks in 1910 to more than 43 percent as the depression got under way.

African Americans frequently expressed their enthusiasm for life in the urban North in biblical terms. They described northern cities as the

With all of their belongings lashed onto their car, a Florida family prepares for the long journey north. During this period, however, most African-American migrants traveled by train.

A panel from painter Jacob Lawrence's 1940–41 series, Migrations of the Negro.

"Promised Land" and "Land of Hope" and the trip north as the "Flight from Egypt." When a trainload of blacks crossed the Ohio River on their way north, they knelt down to pray and sang the hymn "I Done Come Out of the Land of Egypt with the Good News." One black migrant to Chicago wrote back to his southern home: "The [colored] men are making good." A woman wrote back from the same city: "I am well and thankful to say I am doing well. . . . I work in Swifts Packing Company." "Up here," another black migrant wrote, "A man can be a man."

Unfortunately, as African Americans entered cities in growing numbers, they faced new problems with inequality. The discriminatory policies of employers, labor unions, and northern city and state governments left African Americans occupying the so-called Negro jobs at the bottom of the urban economy. As one black worker recalled, African American men "were limited, they only did the dirty work. . . . jobs that even Poles didn't want." Some black women also gained jobs in the industrial sector, but most worked in domestic and personal service, as white women gained increasing access to clerical and professional positions.

White workers frequently referred to blacks as a "scab race" (a *scab* was a person who took the job of a worker who was on strike) and used this stereotype to justify the exclusion of blacks from labor unions and better paying skilled jobs. At the same time, segregated neighborhoods emerged, racial violence became common, and African Americans faced increasing restrictions on where they could live, the places they could go for entertainment and leisure, and the schools they and their children could attend.

Despite stiff barriers to their progress, African Americans developed energetic responses to the new urban environment. As their numbers increased, black workers played a crucial role in shaping African-American reactions to the city. They not only helped to create the new urban gospel and blues music but established the foundations for the rise of a new black business and professional middle class. Black professionals offered services in law, medicine, dentistry, journalism, and music, while black business people established new insurance, real

Scholar and civil rights activist W. E. B. Du Bois (1868–1963) devoted his life to the cause of achieving equal rights for blacks. Following the end of World War I, Du Bois wrote in a Crisis *magazine editorial, "We return. We return from fighting. We return fighting. Make way for Democracy! We saved it in France, and by the great Jehovah, we will save it in the U.S.A, or know the reason why."*

estate, restaurant, cosmetic, boarding, recreational, and sports establishments, including professional baseball teams such as the Homestead Grays in Pittsburgh and the Monarchs of Kansas City.

Referring to themselves as "New Negroes," African Americans also made new demands for full access to the fruits of American citizenship and democracy. During the 1920s, the voice of the "New Negroes" was expressed in a broad range of political, economic, and cultural activities. W. E. B. Du Bois, James Weldon Johnson, and the National Association for the Advancement of Colored People (NAACP) demanded equal rights for black people as citizens. Ida B. Wells-Barnett, Mary Church Terrell, and other militant anti-lynching crusaders reinforced the NAACP's campaign for full citizenship and equal protection under the law. Alain Locke, the magazine *New Negro*, and the arts and ideas of the Harlem Renaissance gave the black quest for citizenship literary expression on a nationwide scale.

On the other hand, some voices revealed class divisions and social conflicts within the black community. A. Philip Randolph, Milton P. Webster, and others in the Brotherhood of Sleeping Car Porters and Maids insisted that black workers unite and demand inclusion in the organized "house of labor." Such leaders felt that Brotherhood members should consider themselves part of a larger multiracial working class whose interests transcended the boundaries of any one race. For their part, Marcus M. Garvey, the Universal Negro Improvement Association, and the Back to Africa movement also appealed to the black masses. The

Marcus Garvey (1887–1940), the founder of the Universal Negro Improvement Association, attracted millions of followers in the early 1920s with his fiery oratory and his calls for worldwide unity among blacks.

Garvey movement pressed for a separate and independent existence for blacks. Garvey emphasized the need for "race pride" and developed the ideology of pan-Africanism, which stressed the kinship of African peoples around the globe.

The social movements of the 1920s signaled the dawn of a new day in black politics and the struggle for equal rights. When blacks in Chicago helped to elect Oscar DePriest to the U.S. Congress in 1928, they gave an early indication of the resurgence of African-American influence in local, state, and national politics. The last black U.S. congressman, George L. White of North Carolina, had left office in 1901. Upon stepping down from the House he had predicted that "Phoenixlike" African Americans would "rise up someday and come again" to the U.S. Congress and to a fuller integration into American society that had been promised but not delivered during the period of Reconstruction after the Civil War.

Although black political culture reflected the growing segregation of blacks in the cities, African Americans retained a core of white allies. Interracial alliances helped fuel the expansion of social welfare and civil rights organizations such as the National Urban League, NAACP, and Commission on Interracial Cooperation. Black-white cooperation was most apparent in the crusade against lynchings, disfranchisement (obstacles designed to thwart the right of blacks to vote), and racial discrimination in social services.

But African Americans soon faced the bitter and unequal impact of the Great Depression. It was during this time of hardship and despair that the black community came together to support the causes of racial and social justice being put forward by the social welfare programs of the New Deal and the vigorous protest movements organized by the most radical of the nation's unions.

CHAPTER 1

AN OLD DEAL, 1929–1934

◇ ◇ ◇

Long before the stock market crash in October 1929, African Americans had experienced hard times. The "last hired and the first fired," African Americans entered the Great Depression earlier and more deeply than other racial and ethnic groups. Sociologists St. Clair Drake and Horace R. Cayton believed that the black community served as a "barometer sensitive to the approaching storm." Months before the stock market crash, the *Chicago Defender* warned that "something is happening . . . and it should no longer go unnoticed. During the past three weeks hardly a day has ended that there has not been a report of another firm discharging its employees, many of whom have been faithful workers at these places for years." As late as 1934, an unemployed black worker spoke for many when he appealed to the NAACP for help to feed and clothe his family. "I am writing you asking if you will assist me in procuring work . . . or Direct Relief. . . . I need food and raiment for my wife and children."

The depression brought mass suffering to the country as a whole. National income dropped by nearly 50 percent, from $81 billion in 1929 to $40 billion in 1932; unemployment rose to an estimated 25 percent of the labor force; and nearly 20 million Americans turned to public and private relief agencies to prevent starvation and destitution. Still, African Americans suffered more than their white counterparts, received less from their government, and got what they called a "raw deal" rather than a "new deal."

With all of their possessions in their arms, this couple from Arkansas hits the road in search of work. The Great Depression struck African Americans especially hard.

Cotton pickers at work in South Carolina. As the price of cotton plummeted during the depression, it became harder and harder for black farmers to support themselves.

The depression took its toll on virtually every facet of African-American life. As unemployment rose, membership in churches, clubs, and fraternal orders dropped. Blacks frequently related the pain of this separation from friends and acquaintances. "I used to belong to a Baptist church, but don't go there now. I can't go anywhere looking like this." "I

Cotton pickers in Pulaski County, Arkansas, gather before beginning their day's work. "I keep on messin' around on the farm," one sharecropper told a WPA interviewer, "but I tell my son-in-law to keep on public work 'cause there ain't no money in farming."

don't attend church as often as I used to. You know I am not fixed like I want to be—haven't got the clothes I need."

Blacks in the rural South faced the most devastating impact of the Great Depression. As cotton prices dropped from 18 cents per pound to less than 6 cents by early 1933, an estimated 2 million black farmers faced hard times. The number of black sharecroppers dropped from nearly 392,000 in 1930 to less than 300,000 as the depression spread. All categories of rural black labor—landowners, cash tenants (those renting land for a fixed amount), sharecroppers (those working land in exchange for a percentage of the crop), and wage laborers—suffered from declining incomes. Mechanical devices had already reduced the number of workers needed for plowing, hoeing, and weeding, but planters now experimented with mechanical cotton pickers as well. As one black woman put it, many jobs had "gone to machines, gone to white people, or gone out of style." The novelist Richard Wright reinforced the point in a photographic essay on the period: "As plantation after plantation fails, the Bosses of the Buildings [northern industrialists] acquire control and send

tractors upon the land, and still more of us are compelled to search for 'another place.'" Public and private relief efforts were virtually non-existent in the rural South, forcing farm families to continue their trek to the city.

Despite declining opportunities to work in southern and northern cities, black migration continued during the depression years. The percentage of urban blacks rose from about 44 percent in 1930 to nearly 50 percent during the depression years. The black population in northern cities increased by nearly 25 percent; the number of cities with black populations of more than 100,000 increased from 1 in 1930 to 11 in 1935. Public social services played an increasing role in decisions to move. As the Swedish economist Gunnar Myrdal noted in *An American Dilemma*, his classic study of black life during the period, "It was much harder for Negroes who needed it to get relief in the South than in the North."

Black longshoremen in Virginia take a break from their work. As the unemployment rate for blacks in urban areas rose, competition for scarce jobs became fierce. Unscrupulous white foremen often took advantage of this situation by demanding kickbacks from workers.

The increasing migration of blacks to cities intensified the poverty of established residents. Before the stock market crash of 1929, urban blacks had already faced the impact of increasing mechanization (machines replacing humans in the workplace), declining demand for manufactured goods, and loss of employment to whites. The stock market crash further undercut the economic position of African Americans. By 1932, black urban unemployment reached well over 50 percent, more than twice the rate of whites. In northern and southern cities, black workers faced special difficulties trying to hold on to their jobs. In Pittsburgh, for example, some black workers were fired when they refused to give kickbacks to the foreman for being permitted to keep their jobs. "I was just laid off—why? Because I wouldn't pay off the foreman. He knows us colored folks has to put up with everything to keep a job so he asks for two-three dollars anytime an' if you don't pay, you get a poor payin' job or a lay-off." Other black workers expressed the same grievance. "My division foreman charged me $20 one time for taking me back on, after he had laid me off; then asked me for $15 more after I had worked a while. I just got tired of that way of doin' and wouldn't pay him; now I'm out of a job." At the same time, unemployed whites made increasing inroads on the so-called "Negro jobs," lower-level positions that blacks had occupied during good times. Not only in factories but in street cleaning, garbage collection, and domestic service work, whites competed for the traditionally black jobs.

As the depression intensified, many white women entered the labor force for the first time. They competed with black women for jobs as maids, cooks, and housekeepers. In northern cities, unemployment and destitution forced many black women to participate in the notorious "slave market." Congregating on the sidewalks of major cities, these women offered their services to white women, who drove up in their cars seeking domestic help. Some of the employers were working-class women themselves and paid as little as five dollars weekly for full-time household workers. In their observations of the practice in the Bronx, New York, two black women, Ella Baker and Marvel Cooke, compared the practice to the treatment of slaves in *Uncle Tom's Cabin,* Harriet Beecher Stowe's 1852 novel: "She who is fortunate (?) enough to please Mrs. Simon Legree's scrutinizing eye is led away to perform hours of multifarious household drudgeries. Under a rigid watch, she is permitted to scrub floors on her bended knees, to hang precariously from window sills, cleaning window after window, or to strain and sweat over steaming tubs of heavy blankets, spreads and furniture covers." The work was difficult indeed. One young black woman, Millie Jones, offered a detailed description of her work for one family for five dollars a week.

> Did I have to work? and how! For five bucks and car fare a week. . . . Each and every week, believe it or not, I had to wash every one of those windows [15 in a six-room apartment]. If that old hag found as much as the teeniest speck on any one of 'em, she'd make me do it over. I guess I would do anything rather than wash windows. On Mondays I washed and did as much of the ironing as I could. The rest waited over for Tuesday. There were two grown sons in the family and her husband. That meant that I would have at least twenty-one shirts to do every week. Yeah, and ten sheets and at least two blankets, besides. They all had to be done just so, too. Gosh, she was a particular woman.

Making matters worse, many employers cheated the women out of their wages. As Baker and Cooke put it, "Fortunate, indeed, is she who

The Great Depression forced growing numbers of white women to enter the work force, where they competed with black women for jobs. Here, blacks and whites work side by side at a cannery in North Carolina.

Many urban black women found work as domestic servants. Such jobs might pay as little as five dollars for a week of full-time work.

gets the full hourly rate promised. Often, her day's slavery is rewarded with a single dollar bill or whatever her unscrupulous employer pleases to pay. More often, the clock is set back for an hour or more. Too often she is sent away without any pay at all." In urban factories and commercial laundries, black women also faced difficult times. In a New York laundry, black women worked 50 hours each week. According to one employee, "It was speed up, speed up, eating lunch on the fly." Women working in the starching department stood on their feet for 10 hours each day, "sticking their hands into almost boiling starch." When the employees complained, the boss threatened to fire and replace them with workers from the large pool of unemployed women. But black women did not accept these conditions without a fight.

Racism and job competition helped to narrow the margin between bare survival and destitution. Evidence of racism abounded. In the South, white workers rallied around such slogans as "No Jobs for Niggers Until Every White Man Has a Job" and "Niggers, back to the cotton

Black women faced difficult and dangerous conditions in urban factories. Here, women cut fish in a North Carolina plant, where the employer's demand for speed could result in accidents involving the loss of fingers.

fields—city jobs are for white folks." The most violent efforts to displace black workers occurred on southern railroads, where the white brotherhoods, as their unions were called, intimidated, attacked, and murdered black workers in order to take their jobs. One contemporary observer, journalist Hilton Butler, offered a list of black firemen who lost their lives or were seriously injured: "Gus Emera, Negro fireman at Durant, saw a closed car rush toward him as he stepped from an engine to a side track. He jumped back in time to miss the second shotgun load, but the first was sufficient to send him to the railroad hospital with serious wounds.—Cleve Sims, fireman also stationed at Durant, walked into the yards at night to go to work. From behind a water tank a shotgun blazed, and Cleve fell badly wounded." By early 1933, nearly a dozen black firemen had lost their lives in various parts of the country. Although the Ku Klux Klan, a violent white supremacist organization, had declined by the mid-1920s, it now renewed its attacks on African Americans. Butler concluded: "Dust had been blown from the shotgun, the whip, and the noose, and Ku Klux Klan practices were being resumed in the certainty that dead men not only tell no tales but create vacancies."

The discriminatory policies of employers and labor unions also affected African Americans in northern cities. Employers maintained their views that African Americans were fit only for dirty, unpleasant, low paying, and heavy work. As blacks sought employment, employers again frequently claimed, "We don't have a foundry in our plant and that's the kind of work Negroes are best suited for." In Milwaukee, one firm justified its exclusion of black workers in familial and paternalistic terms: "We just sort of work like a family here and to bring in Negro workers would cause confusion and cause white workers to feel that their jobs

With the dome of the U.S. Capitol visible in the background, members of the Ku Klux Klan march down Pennsylvania Avenue in 1928. During the depression, the Klan stepped up its attacks on blacks, hoping to drive them from the work force.

had lost in dignity if being done by Negroes." White workers supported and frequently demanded such policies. Twenty-four unions, 10 of them affiliates of the American Federation of Labor (AFL), barred blacks completely, and others practiced other forms of discrimination and exclusion. Thus, disproportionately large numbers of African Americans entered the bread lines, sold their belongings, and faced eviction from their homes.

It was a difficult time, but the Republican administration of President Herbert Hoover did little to relieve the suffering. Hoover resisted proposals for aiding the nation's poor and destitute. Instead, he pursued a policy of indirect relief through the establishment of such agencies as the Reconstruction Finance Corporation, which provided loans to relieve the credit problems of huge corporations like railroads, banks, and insurance companies. By "priming the pump" of big business, Hoover believed that federal aid to corporations would stimulate production, create new jobs, and increase consumer spending—that is, that wealth would "trickle down" to the rest of the economy and end the depression. Unfortunately, these policies provided little help to African Americans.

Despite their suffering under the Hoover administration, African Americans rallied to the slogan "Who but Hoover?" in the Presidential election of 1932. Hoover had not only failed to advance effective policies for dealing with the depression; he had also offended African Americans in a variety of ways, including refusing to be photographed with black leaders. Still, he received about 66 percent of the black vote. Only in New York and Kansas City, Missouri, did the majority of blacks vote for Franklin Delano Roosevelt (known as FDR). The Republican party of Abraham Lincoln was still seen as the party of emancipation. Its role in the emancipation, or freeing, of slaves represented a "long memory" for African Americans. Moreover, despite their lowly position, blacks had seen real opportunities open up for them in the industrial expansion of the 1920s. Although skeptical, some blacks took heart in Hoover's words that "we in America today are nearer to the final triumph over poverty than ever before in the history of any land. The poorhouse is vanishing from us."

From the black vantage point Roosevelt looked little better than Hoover. As assistant secretary of the navy during World War I, he had supported the racial segregation of the armed forces. He had also adopted Warm Springs, Georgia, as his second home and accepted the

A PROGRESSIVE CANDIDATE
WITH CONSTRUCTIVE POLICIES
FOR **PRESIDENT**

GOVERNOR
FRANKLIN D. ROOSEVELT

OF NEW YORK

A poster from the 1932 Presidential campaign of Franklin D. Roosevelt. Roosevelt won the election even though 66 percent of blacks voted for his opponent, incumbent President Herbert Hoover.

system of racial segregation in that state. Moreover, during its national convention the Democratic party rejected an NAACP proposal for a civil rights plank that called for an end to racial discrimination. Thus, for a variety of reasons, African Americans were not inclined to support FDR over Hoover.

But FDR won the election, and once in office he did little to build confidence among African Americans. The new President depended on southern segregationists to pass and implement his "New Deal" programs. FDR saw the depression as an economic disaster that required massive federal aid and planning. The President formulated his New Deal programs accordingly, giving close attention to the needs of big business, agriculture, and labor. Roosevelt opposed federal antilynching legislation, prevented black delegations from visiting the White House, and refused to make civil rights and racial equality a priority.

FDR repeatedly justified his actions on the grounds that he needed southern white support for his economic relief and recovery programs. In a conversation with an NAACP official, he confided, "If I come out for the antilynching bill now, they will block every bill I ask Congress to pass to keep America from collapsing. I just can't take that risk."

African-American rights were placed on hold. Each piece of New Deal legislation failed to safeguard African Americans against racial discrimination. The National Recovery Administration (NRA), Agricultural Adjustment Administration (AAA), the Works Progress [later Projects] Administration (WPA), the Tennessee Valley Authority (TVA), the Civilian Conservation Corps (CCC), and the Federal Emergency

Black women work at a mattress factory in Pensacola, Florida, supported by the Federal Emergency Relief Administration. Because their rates of unemployment and poverty were much higher than those of whites, African Americans received a disproportionately large number of public works jobs, but at less pay than whites.

Relief Administration (FERA), to name only a few, all left blacks vulnerable to discriminatory employers, agency officials, and local whites. Despite the initiation of New Deal relief measures, African Americans repeatedly complained of their inability to secure relief. When a father of six lost his job and sought relief in the city of Pittsburgh, relief officials denied his request. Only when he deserted his family, his wife reported, did she and the children receive aid. According to the woman's testimony: "He told me once that if he wasn't living at home the welfare people would help me and the kids, and maybe he just went away on that account." Southern state and local officials disregarded federal guidelines and paid African-American relief recipients less than their white counterparts. In Atlanta, blacks on relief received an average of $19.29 per month compared to $32.66 for whites. In Jacksonville, Florida, about 5,000 whites received 45 percent of the relief funds, while the 15,000 blacks on relief received the remaining 55 percent. Southern politicians defended the practice, arguing that the low living standards of blacks enabled them to live on less than whites. One black man in Louisiana complained to the NAACP:

> I have been deprived of work since Oct. 20th 1933. . . . Being denied of work so long I was forced to apply for direct relief and the woman Parrish director of the [F.]E.R.A. told me because I had quit a job in Sept. that only paid me $2.00 per week 10–14 hours per day and because I had written several letters to Washington reporting this office she said you will not get any direct relief here. I will show you that you cannot run this office [she said].

And a letter from Alabama told the same tale:

> N.A.A.C.P. Dear Sir—Please allow me to present a question to you which myself is very important because I am one of families that is in very bad need of aid an up to this date have been denied so it have retch the stage that something must be did. It is a well known fact that one cannot live without

Unemployed blacks line up outside the State Employment Service in Memphis, Tennessee, in 1938. During the depression black relief recipients received far less aid than their white counterparts.

food and clothes so a friend and myself being among the unemployed and is not getting any aid so far from the public welfare of this county is asking for aid or information about aid from some source. Will you see after this matter at once . . . Its awful bad to wait for someone who does not care to give you food.

From Georgia, a widow explained the abuse and violence that her 17-year-old son faced when he sought work relief:

Dear Sir—Sometime ago about 6 or 7 weeks ago my boy went up in town to sign to get on the releaf work to get some of the govnor money he was out of a job and I am a poor widder woman with a house full of little childrens and a cripple girl to take ceare of they woulden let him sign the white peoples knocked him down run him out of town woulden let him com back to town he went back to town in about 5 weaks they got after him agin about a hundred head of white mens with knives and they run him all ove town they cout him they throwed him in back of a truck hog fashion he got out som way they put a Bulldog on him then he ran in a stor then som of the collord mens beg the cheef police to put him in jale to keep the mob from killing him the cheaff say let them kill him just so they dont mobb him heare in town the night marshell put him in jale for safe keeping and I hade to pay him $5.00 to get him out and he had to leave town dont be see heare no more if they see him enny more they will sure kill him he left in the night walking with no money I wont be able to gave him nothing and I want him to help me that is my sun he is just 17 years old—Just write to help me if you all please take up far me and help me I am his mother.

The local Federal Emergency Relief Administration was not alone in discriminating against blacks. The Agricultural Adjustment Act paid farmers to withdraw cotton-farming land from production, create a shortage, and drive up the price of cotton on the market. Set up to administer the law at the local level, AAA county committees excluded African Americans from participation. By depriving African Americans of representation, white landowners were able to put into place policies that drove black landowners into the ranks of sharecroppers and forced growing numbers of sharecroppers off the land altogether. During its first year, for example, the AAA encouraged farmers to plow under cotton that was already planted. Landowners took government checks, plowed up cotton, and denied tenants a share of the government income.

At the same time that planters removed more acres of land from cultivation, the largest landowners turned increasingly to scientific and mechanized farming. Tractors and cotton-picking machines rendered

While working for the Farm Security Administration in 1936, photographer Dorothea Lange took this picture of a white land owner in Clarksdale, Mississippi, standing in front of a group of black men.

black labor more and more dispensable. Although their numbers dwindled, the remaining black sharecroppers still earned less than their white counterparts. White sharecroppers received an average income of $417 per year compared to only $295 for blacks. White wage hands (those paid hourly wages) received $232 per year, compared to only $175 for blacks.

Lower earnings aggravated other forms of racial inequality. In his survey of 612 black farm families in Macon County, Alabama, the sociologist Charles S. Johnson found that more than half lived in one- and two-room weatherworn shacks. When asked if her house leaked when it rained, a black woman said, "No, it don't leak in here, it just rains in here

35

A black family in Florida called this weather-beaten shack home. Poor black farm families had to improvise when their landlords refused to repair or maintain their homes.

and leaks outdoors." Another tenant complained that the landlord refused to provide lumber for repairs: "All he's give us . . . is a few planks. . . . It's nothin doin'. We just living outdoors." Food was also difficult for farm families to come by. A writer for the magazine *New Republic* reported in 1931 that some black farmers in the cotton region were near starvation: "Some of the men who are plowing are hungry. They don't have enough to eat. . . . And with hunger gnawing at their vitals they plow in earnest, because they are in a desperate situation and they exist in terrible anxiety. So they plow hard." Black tenants had good reason to view these early years of the New Deal with skepticism.

The National Recovery Act also discriminated against black workers. Partly by exempting domestic service and unskilled laborers from its provisions, the NRA removed most blacks from its minimum wage and democratic participatory requirements. Since more than 60 percent of African Americans worked in these sectors, the measure had little meaning for most blacks, especially women. Nonetheless, other blacks who held on to their precarious footing in the industrial labor force, despite hard times, faced new pressures from employers and white workers. In 1934, the Milwaukee, Wisconsin, Urban League reported a strike at the Wehr Steel Foundry. The chief aim of the strike, the league reported, was the "dismissal of Negroes from the plant." Only the firing of black workers, the League believed, would end the strike. When black workers crossed the picket line, police joined strikers in attacks on them. The Milwaukee Urban League reported that "the first few days of the strike brought considerable violence between the Negroes who attempted to continue on the jobs and the white pickets. . . . Police had been summoned [by management] to protect those who cared to enter but in turn joined with the strikers in overturning an automobile filled with Negro workers."

Even on construction projects for black institutions, white workers rallied to bar African-American workers. In St. Louis, for example, when the General Tile Company hired a black tile setter for the $2 million Homer Phillips Hospital for blacks, all the white AFL union men quit and construction was delayed for two months. In Long Island and Manhattan, the Brotherhood of Electrical Workers and Building Service Employees' Union pursued similar practices. When African Americans were brought under the higher wage provisions of the law in southern textile firms, employers reclassified African-American jobs in order to remove them from the protection of the NRA codes. Some firms simply argued that blacks were less efficient than whites and thus deserved low wages. In Atlanta, for example, the Scripto Manufacturing company told black workers that "this company does not base wages on color but entirely on efficiency. Our records show that the efficiency of colored help is only 50 percent of that of white help in similar plants. . . . If the 'false friends' of the colored people do not stop their propaganda about paying the same wages to colored and white employees this company will be forced to move the factory to a section where the minimum wage will produce the greatest production. *Stop your 'false friends' from talking you out of a job.*"

Where the codes did upgrade the pay of black workers, many firms replaced their African-American work forces with white employees. It is no wonder that blacks frequently called the NRA the "Negro Run Around," "Negroes Ruined Again," and "Negro Rarely Allowed." In short, NRA legislation (particularly section 7a, which gave workers the right to bargain collectively with employers) enabled labor unions to strengthen their hand at the expense of blacks in both North and South. As late as 1935, organized white labor also blocked the inclusion of a nondiscrimination clause in the National Labor Relations Act, sponsored by Senator Robert Wagner of New York. The new Wagner law gave workers and their unions extended protection in their effort to bargain collectively with management. According to Wagner's assistant Leon Kyserling, "The American Federation of Labor fought bitterly to eliminate this clause and much against his will Senator Wagner had to consent to elimination in order to prevent scuttling of the entire bill."

African Americans not only faced discrimination in industrial, agricultural, and relief programs but confronted racial bias in federal housing, Social Security, regional planning, and youth programs as well. The Federal Housing Administration refused to guarantee mortgages (home loans) in racially integrated neighborhoods; the Social Security Act excluded farm laborers and domestic service employees; and the TVA and CCC developed along segregationist and unequal lines.

Established in 1933, the Tennessee Valley Authority was promoted by the Roosevelt administration as a model of social planning that would improve the lives of millions of Americans in seven states in the Tennessee River Valley. It was hoped that the TVA would stimulate economic development and reduce poverty by establishing a massive program of rural electrification at dramatically reduced rates. African Americans comprised 11 percent of the 2 million residents of the region, and the project promised "nondiscrimination" in its official design.

African Americans took heart at the promise of benefits from TVA. Yet the project soon accepted the racial status quo for black workers and their families in the valley. The agency barred blacks from skilled and managerial positions, excluded them from vocational training programs, and reinforced patterns of segregation in housing. When queried about the exclusion of blacks from its model town of Norris, Tennessee, TVA chairman Arthur Morgan referred to a long "lily white" waiting list and suggested that it was unlikely that blacks would be able to move to Norris. Even more important, African Americans received inadequate benefits from the reduced rates for electrical power for their homes. In an essay called "Plight of the Negro in the Tennessee Valley," the NAACP magazine *The Crisis* reported that "for Negroes the introduction of cheaper electric rates into Lee County as a result of the TVA power policy has meant nothing. Landlords, whether of Negro slum dwellers in

For African Americans viewing this cartoon, it would come as no surprise that both the employee and employer reaping the benefits of the National Recovery Act (NRA) were white—because the NRA exempted agricultural and domestic workers from its provisions and therefore offered little or no assistance to blacks.

Tupelo or of Negro tenant farmers in the rural section of the county, have not found it to their advantage to wire their Negro tenants' homes at the cost of $15 to $25, when already they are squeezing all the rent possible from these tenants."

The Civilian Conservation Corps (CCC) established camps to aid unemployed youth. The agency employed young men in the work of con-

A typical—young and white—worker in the Civilian Conservation Corps (CCC) plants trees. African Americans found it difficult to gain CCC jobs.

servation, reforestation, and prevention of soil erosion, but it gave preference to young whites. Even where blacks constituted the majority of the total population—in certain counties of Mississippi and Alabama, for example—they were given fewer than 6 percent of CCC jobs. One contemporary scholar, Arthur Raper, charged that "the CCC has remained a white institution, with no more coloring than landownership, which tolerates the possession of one acre in twenty Negroes." When African Americans did gain employment on CCC projects, they were segregated and treated unfairly compared to whites. In New York, a young black man offered a vivid description of his induction into a CCC camp, which was administered by the U.S. Army:

> According to instructions, I went Monday morning at 8 o'clock to Pier I,
> North River. . . . a group of us marched over to U.S. Army headquarters on

Whitehall Street in charge of an Army officer. Here we stripped for a complete physical examination. Then we were grouped into busloads. We reached Camp Dix [New Jersey] about 7:30 that evening. When my record was taken at Pier I a 'C' was placed on it. When the busloads were made up at Whitehall Street an officer reported as follows: '35, 8 colored' . . . before we left the bus the officer shouted emphatically: 'Colored boys fall out in the rear.' The colored from several buses were herded together, and stood in line until after the white boys had been registered and taken to their tents. . . . This separation of the colored from the whites was complete and rigidly maintained at this camp. . . . Our officers who, of course, are white, are a captain, a first lieutenant, a doctor, and several sergeants.

In the face of blatant forms of discrimination during the early New Deal, African Americans found little to praise in the government's relief efforts. They were acutely aware that they suffered disproportionately from unemployment but faced the greatest discrimination and received the least benefits from government relief, work, housing, and Social Security programs. All Americans gained increasing assistance from the federal government, but such assistance would only slowly reach African Americans and help to reverse the impact of hard times on their families and communities. By the mid-1930s, however, a variety of new forces would gradually transform the "raw deal" into a "new deal."

FARM SECURITY ADMINISTRATION AIDS THE NEGRO FARMER

THE NEGRO FARMER'S PROBLEM IS THE SOUTHERN FARMER'S PROBLEM 95 PERCENT OF NEGRO FARMERS ARE IN THE SOUTH. 47 PERCENT OF THESE ARE SHARECROPPERS. 32 PERCENT ARE TENANTS. — **ONLY 21 PERCENT ARE OWNERS.**

Toward

From

FARM SECURITY HELPS THROUGH ...

1. REHABILITATION LOANS FOR EQUIPMENT, LIVESTOCK, SEED, FERTILIZER.
2. TENANT PURCHASE LOANS TO MAKE OWNERS OUT OF CROPPERS AND TENANTS.
3. DEBT ADJUSTMENT TO REDUCE INTEREST, RE-SCALE PAYMENTS TO THE FARMER'S CAPACITY.
4. CO-OPERATIVE COMMUNITIES TO ENABLE SMALL FARMERS TO COMPETE WITH LARGE, MECHANIZED FARMS.

CHAPTER 2
A NEW DEAL, 1935–1939
◇ ◇ ◇

B etween the stock market crash of 1929 and the early years
of the New Deal, the condition of African Americans
moved from bad to worse. Neither the Hoover administration nor the first efforts of the new Democratic regime of
Franklin Roosevelt did much to lessen the suffering of
African Americans. By 1935, however, a variety of forces helped to transform the relationship between blacks and the New Deal. Changes in
American attitudes toward race and class, the emergence of new interracial alliances, and the growing political mobilization of African Americans themselves all put pressure on the federal government to address
the needs of African Americans. In a nationwide radio broadcast, President Franklin D. Roosevelt symbolized the shift. In a speech before a
conference of the Churches of Christ in America, he condemned lynching as murder: "Lynch law is murder, a deliberate and definite
disobedience of the high command, 'Thou shalt not kill.' We do not ex-
cuse those in high places or low who condone lynch law." Following the
President's pronouncement, in January 1934 the NAACP's *Crisis* magazine exclaimed that FDR was the only President to declare "frankly that
lynching is murder. We all knew it, but it is unusual to have a president
of the United States admit it. These things give us hope."

As the federal government increasingly affirmed its responsibility
for the social welfare of all Americans, it helped to change the context of
the African-American struggle for social justice. By 1939, African Americans had gradually gained a larger share of New Deal social programs

*The Farm Security
Administration high-
lights its efforts to aid
black farmers in this
1939 poster. The FSA
sought to increase the
number of black farm-
ers who owned the
land they worked.*

and improved their economic situation. African-American income from New Deal work and relief programs—the Public Works Administration (PWA), Works Progress Administration (WPA), and Civilian Conservation Corps (CCC)—now nearly equaled their income from employment in agriculture and domestic service. On CCC projects, African Americans increased their presence from less than 6 percent of the work force in 1935 to 11 percent in 1939. African Americans also occupied about one-third of all low-income PWA housing units, obtained a rising share of Federal Farm Security loans, and gained access to a variety of new WPA educational and cultural programs. Because the government spent more money on education, including the building of new facilities, black illiteracy dropped 10 percent during the 1930s. The number of African Americans on relief and the amount of money available to them rose steadily. African Americans increasingly hailed such New Deal social programs as a "godsend." Some even suggested that God "will lead me" but relief "will feed me." African Americans now perceived that a "new deal" was truly in the making.

A smiling couple moves into their new home in a government-sponsored housing project in Newport News, Virginia, in 1937.

President Franklin Roosevelt responded to the growing importance of the black vote in national elections by appointing increasing numbers of blacks to federal posts. Members of the "Black Cabinet," as these appointees came to be called, gathered for a photograph in 1938.

The changing relationship between blacks and the New Deal was not merely a matter of the government's shifting attitude toward the social welfare of all Americans. The Roosevelt administration also responded to the growing impact of the black vote on national elections, the emergence of an interracial alliance of black and white New Dealers, and especially a rising core of black federal appointees. Roosevelt reacted to the growing importance of the black vote by appointing increasing numbers of African Americans to federal posts. By the mid-1930s, some 45 blacks had received appointments in various New Deal agencies and cabinet departments. The "Black Cabinet," as these black advisers were called, included Robert L. Vann, editor of the *Pittsburgh Courier,* in the Office of the Attorney General; William H. Hastie, a civil rights attorney, in the Department of the Interior; Robert C. Weaver, an economist, also in the Interior Department; Lawrence A. Oxley, a social worker, in the Department of Labor; Edgar Brown, president of the United Government Employees, in the Civilian Conservation Corps; and Mary McLeod Bethune, founder of Bethune-Cookman College, head of the Negro Division of the National Youth Administration. The "Black Cabinet" enabled African Americans to improve their position in a variety of New Deal programs.

The First Lady, Eleanor Roosevelt, played a key role in helping these black New Dealers improve the federal response to the needs of African Americans. Although Mrs. Roosevelt had little contact with

45

As secretary of the interior and administrator of the Public Works Administration, Harold Ickes (seated between FDR and Vice President Henry Wallace) sought to ensure that blacks were not denied the benefits of New Deal programs.

African Americans before early 1933, she soon befriended Walter White of the NAACP and Mary McLeod Bethune. Through her frequent interactions with black leaders, Eleanor Roosevelt gradually increased her support of civil rights issues. Following the election of 1936, for example, she endorsed legislation designed to abolish the poll tax (which denied blacks the right to vote by establishing discriminatory financial requirements), make lynching a federal offense, and increase aid to black institutions, particularly schools. Historians credit Mrs. Roosevelt with helping to push FDR's position on civil rights from one of caution and aloofness to one of significant support. FDR eventually allowed himself to be photographed with black leaders, conferred with civil rights delegations at the White House, and sent greetings to African-American organizations.

As the White House seemed to increase its support for racial justice, other New Dealers took heart and advanced the cause of African Americans, too. The policies of Harold Ickes, secretary of the interior and administrator of the PWA; Harry Hopkins, head of the WPA; and a few others exemplified the growing support that African Americans received in some New Deal agencies. Before taking his post as secretary of

Richard Wright was one of many young African-American writers who received support and training from the Federal Writers' Project in the 1930s. His most important work, the novel Native Son *(1940), told the story of Bigger Thomas, a black man in Chicago struggling against a racist society.*

the interior, Ickes had served as president of the Chicago chapter of the NAACP. Upon assuming his government duties, he ended segregation in the department's rest rooms and cafeteria. Although local whites often ignored his policies, Ickes advocated the employment of skilled and unskilled black laborers on PWA construction projects. The secretary insisted that all PWA contractors agree to hire blacks in proportion to their percentage in the 1930 occupational census.

Under the leadership of Harry Hopkins, the WPA established policies making it illegal for any relief official to discriminate "on account of race, creed, or color." FDR had strengthened his hand by issuing Executive Order 7046, which ordered the WPA to assign persons "qualified by training and experience" to work on projects without discrimination "on any grounds whatsoever."

Under Hopkins's leadership, the WPA also promoted black adult education, hired unemployed black professionals, and stimulated the arts within the black community. The WPA education program employed more than 5,000 blacks as leaders and supervisors, taught nearly 250,000 blacks to read and write, and trained many for skilled jobs. The Federal Music Project staged concerts including the works of black composers; the Federal Art Project employed hundreds of black artists; and, under the direction of Hallie Flanagan, the Federal Theater Project (FTP) established an African-American unit. The African-American theater division employed about 500 blacks in New York, developed dramatic productions on African-American life and history, and carried shows to black communities across the country.

Supplementing the artistic work of the FTP was the Federal
Writers' Project (FWP). Young writers and scholars such as St. Clair
Drake, Horace R. Cayton, Richard Wright, and Ralph Ellison gained
opportunities and early training on the Federal Writers' Project. Both
the FWP and FTP developed activities designed to increase interracial
understanding, which in 1938 provoked an investigation by the U.S.
House of Representatives Un-American Activities Committee (HUAC).
The HUAC helped to undercut the growth of these programs by
charging them with "conspiracy and subversion" of American ideas,
beliefs, and institutions.

Although most southern New Dealers resisted equal treatment
for blacks, others supported efforts to improve the status of African
Americans. Born in Alabama, Aubrey Willis Williams served as Deputy
Works Progress Administrator and head of the National Youth Administration (NYA). At the NYA, Williams resisted the establishment of racial
differentials in wages paid to blacks and whites. He repeatedly stated the
belief that African-American youth should be prepared for jobs that
would move them beyond the usual categories of maid and janitor. Will
Alexander, director of the Farm Security Administration (FSA), was another southern white who befriended African Americans during the
period. Under his leadership, the FSA appointed a larger percentage of
black supervisors than any other agency and gradually improved benefits
for African Americans.

There were other reasons why federal policies toward blacks began
to change for the better. Across the land, American attitudes toward race
and class had begun to change. This was reflected in the emergence of
new social, intellectual, cultural, and political currents. Increasing numbers of Americans criticized industrial elites (that is, corporate execu-
tives, bankers, and Wall Street financiers) for eliminating their jobs and
placing them in bread lines. Working Americans launched mass movements for greater government support of their interests during the 1930s.
This increased activism could be seen in the rise of the Communist
party, the resurgence of organized labor, and greater efforts to attract
African Americans to the ranks of both of these types of organizations.

An unpopular minority, the Communist party was especially eager
to attract black members. Although the party often used the race issue to
advance its own agenda of ideological attacks on capitalist institutions,

The Negro Repertory
Company of the Fed-
eral Theater Project
staged an all-black
production of George
Bernard Shaw's
Androcles and
the Lion.

such as the two-party system, it nonetheless played a key role in publicizing racial injustice and placing the issue of civil rights before the nation.

Few blacks joined the Communist party, but its activities on behalf of African Americans soon got their attention. The party's most famous campaigns centered on efforts to free one of its own members, the black Communist Angelo Herndon, from a Georgia chain gang and the attempt to win acquittal on rape charges for nine blacks held in Scottsboro, Alabama, known as the Scottsboro Boys.

The case of the Scottsboro Boys was perhaps the most infamous instance of racial injustice in the courts of the 1930s. During the depression years, blacks and whites routinely "hoboed" the nation's freight trains, traveling from place to place looking for work and the means to survive. In March 1931, a group of black and white youths boarded a freight train southbound from Chattanooga, Tennessee, to Alabama. A fight eventually broke out and the blacks forced the whites off the train. One of the young black men later vividly recalled that day:

> The freight train leaving out of Chattanooga, going around the mountain curves and hills of Tennessee into Alabama, it went so slow anyone could get off and back on. That gave the white boys the idea they could jump off the train and pick up rocks, carry them back on, and chunk them at us Negro boys. The trouble began when three or four white boys crossed over the oil tanker that four of us colored fellows from Chattanooga were in. One of the white boys, he stepped on my hand liked to have knocked me off the train. I didn't say anything then, but the same guy, he brushed by me again and liked to have pushed me off the car. I caught hold of the side of the tanker to keep from falling off. I made a complaint about it and the white boy talked back— mean, serious, white folks Southern talk. That is how the Scottsboro case began . . . with a white foot on my black hand. . . . I don't argue with people. I show them. And I started to show those white boys. The other colored guys, they pitched in on these rock throwers too. Pretty quick the white boys began to lose in the fist fighting. We outmanned them in hand-to-hand scuffling. Some of them jumped off and some we put off. The train, picking up a little speed, that helped us do the job. A few wanted to put up a fight but they didn't have a chance. We had color anger on our side.

The white youths reported the incident to local authorities, who stopped the train near Scottsboro, Alabama. Nine young black men and two white women were removed from the train by the local sheriff. Fearing arrest, the young women accused the black youths of rape at knife point.

Members of the Alabama militia guard the nine Scottsboro Boys as they enter the courthouse. An all-white jury found the group guilty of rape in 1931, sparking protests across the country. Despite these efforts and two U.S. Supreme Court decisions ordering retrials, it took more than 15 years for the last Scottsboro Boy to be released from prison.

Although the black defendants pleaded "not guilty," the court failed to appoint proper legal representation for the young men. An all-white jury ignored the different versions of the events on the train given in the testimony of the women and found the defendants guilty of rape, and the court sentenced all but the youngest to death in the electric chair.

The Communist party soon took up the case. The party's Central Committee issued a statement describing the sentence as a "legal lynching," and within a few days it launched an international crusade to save the young men. As protest rallies emerged in major cities across the nation, non-Communist organizations like the NAACP soon joined communists in demanding justice. At the same time, the party's International Labor Defense pressed the legal case through the Alabama Supreme Court, which upheld the convictions. On two separate occasions the party carried the case forward to the U.S. Supreme Court, which overturned the convictions and ordered retrials, which in both cases, *Powell* v. *Alabama* (1932) and *Norris* v. *Alabama* (1935), led not to release but to new death sentences. However, the execution dates kept being postponed and eventually all defendants were cleared of the charges brought against them. After having spent more than 15 years in jail for a crime he did not commit, the last defendant was released after World War II.

The Communist party not only staged demonstrations and legal actions to free blacks like Herndon and the Scottsboro Boys, it also carried out day-to-day activities designed to improve the economic status of African Americans. The party organized hunger marches, unemployed councils, farm labor unions, and rent strikes to aid unemployed and destitute workers. In Chicago, when families received eviction notices, mothers would sometimes shout to the children, "Run quick find the Reds!" On one occasion, when Communists attempted to prevent the eviction of a black family in Chicago, police shot and killed three African Americans. The Communist party responded by distributing nearly 5,000 leaflets urging black and white workers to unite and demand justice for the deceased. Nearly 50,000 people lined State Street for the funeral procession.

The Communist party also placed blacks in key leadership positions, condemned racial intolerance within its ranks, and conducted public mock trials to dramatize its stand against racism. Nearly 15,000 people attended the trial of August Yokinen in Harlem. Accused of treating blacks with disdain, Yokinen was expelled from the party but, by serving in the civil rights struggle of the black community, he was given an opportunity for readmission.

Black newspaper editors frequently praised the Communists for their work on behalf of African-American rights. One black newspaper editor, William Kelley of the *Amsterdam News*, spoke for many when he concluded that "a little less than a year ago . . . I was suspicious of these gift-bearing Reds . . . lest they should rise to power on the backs of American Negroes and then leave them to their fate. Since that time, a lot of water has run under the bridge, enough to cause us to reevaluate the accomplishments of their movement in our cause . . . the fight that they are putting up . . . strike[s] forcefully at the fundamental wrongs suffered by the Negro today."

During the 1930s the Socialist party also campaigned against racial injustice. In 1929, the party established the United Colored Socialists of America. Socialist party head Norman Thomas appointed a special black organizer for the South and supported a resolution condemning racial discrimination by trade unions. By 1933 the Socialist party endorsed federal antilynching and anti–poll tax legislation; the party also organized sharecroppers' unions and elevated blacks to leadership positions.

In 1932 the Communist party chose James W. Ford to be its candidate for Vice President in the national election. As this fundraising letter, with its prominently featured picture of Ford, shows, the Communist party placed blacks in prominent leadership positions in the hope of attracting large numbers of them to the cause.

THE
FOSTER and FORD————
————————COMMITTEE

35 East 12th Street, Room 909, New York, N. Y.

ALgonquin 4-2215, Ext. 16

September,
1 9 3 2.

WM. Z. FOSTER
For President

JAMES W. FORD
For Vice-President

Dear Friend,

      The undersigned, a group of educators, writers, architects, artists, and professionals in general, have drawn up the enclosed state-ment in support of Wm. Z. Foster and James W. Ford, Communist candidates in the national election campaign.

      We feel that it is essential at this time for all American intellectuals to express their strong dissatisfaction with conditions as they are, and to give impetus to the only group of workers in the American labor movement who are intelligent and brave enough to fight militantly the powers in control.

      The two major parties, we all agree, are hopeless. The Socialist Party, with its present leadership of nice people, does not symbolize change, or a leadership feared by the intrenched class. And the Socialists' persistent attacks on the Soviet Union during its pre-sent bitterest years of struggle, deserve sharp rebuke and repudiation.

      We may not all agree with all the ideas of Communism, but the Communist Party is the only party today feared by the ruling class, and the only party we can vote for that will <u>effectively</u> register our protest against the present economic and political regime.

      Will you join us?

      Please sign the enclosed statement, and mail <u>immediately</u> in the self-addressed envelope.

                Sincerely yours,

            The Foster and Ford Committee

P.S. If you know of any people whose names will lend value to this
      statement, won't you ask them to join you, or write us, and we
      will forward them a similar letter.

The Southern Tenant Farmers Union, led by H. L. Mitchell—shown here at union headquarters in Memphis, Tennessee, in 1938—worked to protect the rights of southern sharecroppers, both black and white.

Launched in 1934, the Southern Tenant Farmers Union (STFU) represented the Socialist party's strongest effort to organize workers across racial lines. Founded near the town of Tyronza, Arkansas, the STFU resolved to organize black and white tenant farmers in the same union. Under the leadership of H. L. Mitchell, a white associate of Norman Thomas, and two ministers, Howard Lester and Claude Williams, the organization advocated economic justice for all sharecroppers and racial justice for African Americans. A white organizer for the STFU emphasized the futility of separate organizations and appealed to what he called "belly hunger" to help erase the color line among farmers. "If we organize only a Union of Negro sharecroppers then the Negroes will be evicted and white sharecroppers from the hill country or the unemployed in Memphis will take their places. If on the other hand we organize only a Union of white sharecroppers, then the white men will be evicted and Negro sharecroppers from Mississippi and the unemployed in Memphis will take their places." Although the organization failed to bring landowners to the bargaining table, it demonstrated how the American left pushed the Roosevelt administration to create a "new deal."

The economic slump of the 1930s and the Roosevelt administration's liberalized labor laws energized the organized labor movement. However, the movement split over the issue of whether to organize workers along broad industrial lines (ignoring the particular craft a worker was engaged in) or on a narrow, craft-by-craft basis. Impatient with the exclusionary policies of the American Federation of Labor (AFL), the Committee for Industrial Organization broke from the AFL at the 1935 convention. Under the leadership of John L. Lewis, head of the United Mine Workers of America (UMW), the CIO (renamed the Congress of Industrial Organizations in 1938) embarked upon an aggressive organizing drive. This change was especially significant for blacks because they were disproportionately represented in mass production industries.

Learning from its failure to organize southern black miners in the coal strikes of 1927, the UMW made a firm commitment to organize both black and white workers. Following the "UMW formula," the CIO soon

Iron ore miners in Jefferson County, Alabama, in 1937. As the number of blacks in mass production industries increased during the 1930s, they were aggressively courted by labor unions hoping to increase their strength.

A steelworker sits outside his union's office in Midland, Pennsylvania, in 1938. The sign in the window gives notice of an important meeting for "members in good standing only."

launched the Steel Workers Organizing Committee (SWOC), the Packinghouse Workers Organizing Committee (PWOC), and the United Automobile Workers (UAW). In each case, the union appealed to black organizations like the NAACP and the National Urban League, employed black organizers, placed African Americans in key union offices, and advocated an end to racially biased pay scales. Under the prodding of black labor leaders like A. Philip Randolph, competition from the emerging CIO, and the growing influence of blacks in the New Deal political coalition, the AFL also modified its position on organizing black workers. AFL president William Green eventually supported the move to free Angelo Herndon and the Scottsboro Boys, to obtain federal antilynching legislation, and to abolish the poll taxes that disenfranchised black voters. By 1939, African Americans had moved into the meeting rooms of the "house of labor."

Reinforcing the lowering of racial barriers in the labor movement were new intellectual and cultural perspectives on race in American society. Scholars, artists, and the popular media gradually changed their views on race. Social scientists rejected the notion of the inborn inferiority of nonwhite races and developed a new consensus. Most intellectuals and social scientists agreed that African Americans were not inferior to whites, that racism injured its victims both psychologically and socially, and that racism itself was a mental illness that damaged the health of the individual and the nation as a whole. These views gained currency in the ongoing research of Columbia University anthropologist Franz Boas, his students, and associates, who questioned the long-held assumption that racial and ethnic group differences were inherited through the genes. As Boas put it, "Where is the proof of the development of specialized hereditary capacities?" In other words, Boas and his associates challenged the racists to prove that African Americans suffered a lower plane of living because they were intellectually inferior to their white counterparts. In short, he forced the social scientific community, which prided itself on attending to the "facts," to recognize that it had little evidence to support some of its most cherished theories. As one scholar put it, "We do not yet know scientifically what the relative intellectual ability of the various races is. Some different tests, equally valid, might give the Negro a higher score than the white. Until we do know, probably the best thing is to *act* as if all races had equivalent mental ability."

The intellectual assault on racism reached its high point in 1937 when the Carnegie Corporation invited the Swedish economist Gunnar Myrdal to the United States to head "a comprehensive study of the Negro." The Myrdal study resulted in the publication of the monumental *An American Dilemma: The Negro Problem and Modern Democracy* (1944). Myrdal brought together numerous scholars to work on different aspects of race relations. All defined the "Negro problem" as a problem of white racism, immorality, and inequality. *An American Dilemma* concluded that "the American Negro problem is in the heart of the [white] American. It is there that the interracial tension has its focus. It is there that the decisive struggle goes on. This is the central viewpoint of this treatise. Though our study includes economic, social, and political race relations, at bottom our problem is the moral dilemma of the American—the conflict between his moral valuations on various levels of consciousness and generality."

Although legal change came slowly, the U.S. Supreme Court issued several rulings that weakened the hold of racism on American society. In the case of *Pearson* v. *Murray* (1936), legal opinions on race started to change. Donald Murray, a black graduate of Amherst College in Massachusetts, applied for admission to the University of Maryland law school. When the school denied him admission based upon his race, he took the case to court and challenged racial discrimination in graduate education. Like most southern states, Maryland had set up a tuition grant program that "assisted" blacks who sought graduate study and professional training by steering them elsewhere. But the Maryland Court of Appeals ordered the University of Maryland to set up a separate law school for blacks or admit them to the white one. Rather than contesting the court's decision, university officials quietly admitted blacks to the law school. In the case of *Missouri ex rel. Gaines* v. *Canada* (1938), the U.S. Supreme Court reinforced the Maryland precedent by ruling that law schools in the various states had to admit blacks or establish separate law schools.

The courts reinforced these decisions with others that slowly began to help blacks achieve full protection under the law. On two occasions (1932, 1935), the U.S. Supreme Court overruled the Alabama Supreme Court in the Scottsboro case and insisted on due process of law for black defendants. In the case of *Hale* v. *Kentucky* (1938), the court noted the systematic exclusion of blacks from jury service and overturned the conviction of a black man accused of murder. Over the next three years, the U.S. Supreme Court also strengthened the economic position of African Americans. It upheld the right of African Americans to boycott businesses that discriminated in their employment practices, struck down a Georgia peonage law that permitted the virtual enslavement of blacks as sharecroppers, and upheld the elimination of unequal salaries for black and white teachers in Norfolk, Virginia. In short, by 1939 the Court had slowly begun to undermine the historic *Plessy* v. *Ferguson* decision

Despite the many opportunities offered to blacks by the New Deal, this sign for a "colored waiting room" at a bus station in Durham, North Carolina, attests to the racial discrimination that was still a part of daily life for the majority of blacks.

of 1896 that permitted a "separate but equal" society for blacks and whites.

Despite shifting conceptions of race and the New Deal's growing response to the needs of blacks, by 1939 poverty, unemployment, and racial discrimination continued to affect the African-American community. Even the most egalitarian programs experienced a huge gap in policy and practice. The Farm Security Administration, which secured home loans for farm families, operated with limited funds and used a tough credit rating system that disqualified most black tenants and sharecroppers from qualifying for loans. Low-income federal housing programs reinforced the racial segregation of urban communities, adding federal policy to the ongoing historical forces—discriminatory real estate agents, restrictive covenants (regulations in many suburban neighborhoods that required resale of properties only to whites), and white neighborhood opposition—in the rise and expansion of the black ghetto.

The Works Progress Administration established regulations ending racial discrimination in its programs, but southern whites continued to

evade the rules and made it more difficult for blacks than whites to gain adequate public works jobs and relief. Black women faced special forms of discrimination on WPA projects in the South. They were often forced to perform "men's jobs" at a time when white women received jobs defined as "clean" or "easy." In a South Carolina town, a local physician reported that "the Beautification project appears to be 'For Negro Women Only.' This project is a type of work that should be assigned to men. Women are worked in 'gangs' in connection with the City's dump pile, incinerator and ditch piles. Illnesses traced to such exposure as these women must face do not entitle them to medical aid at the expense of the WPA." In Jackson, Mississippi, black women worked under the supervision of armed guards, and in Oklahoma a WPA official closed the government project for black women in order to force them to pick "an abundant cotton crop which is in full picking flower." Equally important, African Americans repeatedly complained of the treatment that they received when applying for aid. As one black woman reported, "When I go to them for help they talk to me like I was a dog."

By the late 1930s, as whites returned to full-time employment in private industry in growing numbers, most blacks continued to depend

Black men and women at work on a Mississippi plantation in 1940. The efforts by administrators of New Deal agencies in Washington to end racial discrimination in government programs were largely ignored by local southern administrators.

on public service and relief programs. Despite the various interracial alliances and growing sensitivity to the destructive impact of class and racial inequality, white Americans continued to insist that their needs be met first. While the CIO helped to organize blacks who were fortunate enough to maintain their jobs during the depression years, as the country lifted itself out of the depression it did little to promote the return to employment of black and white workers in equal numbers. For their part, although the Socialists and Communists helped to change attitudes toward interracial cooperation, the benefits of these efforts remained largely symbolic rather than material. Blacks continued to suffer racial injustice. African Americans, in short, would have to attend to their own interests, unite, and wage an even stronger offensive against the barriers of racial and class inequality.

By the mid-1930s, the earlier "raw deal" was gradually supplanted by a "new deal." African Americans gained increasing consideration in the distribution of federal aid. In their own words and actions, they confirmed the importance of social programs in helping them to cope with hard times. Yet, even as the New Deal aided African Americans in distress, it failed to stimulate economic recovery among the nation's black citizens. New Deal relief, work, and social programs aided African Americans primarily as part of a larger mission to ease destitution among all Americans. Such programs failed to address adequately the issue of racial inequality and the persistence of racial discrimination within and outside government agencies.

The failure of the New Deal to address such issues prolonged and deepened the depression in black communities across the country. This mixed legacy of the New Deal—the persistence of African-American poverty alongside new forms of federal aid—would prompt African Americans to deepen their own unity and struggle even more vigorously in their own behalf. Indeed, from the onset of the Great Depression, African Americans had developed a broad range of creative reactions to hard times. It was in the vigorous defense of their own rights that African Americans would help to usher in a new set of social relations in U.S. society.

YOUTH CONFERENCE *for*
Vocational Opportunity
Sponsored by the
N.Y.A. *and the* URBAN LEAGUE
SAT·APR·2 ND
CENTER AVE. Y.M.C.A.   9 A.M. TO 5 P.M.

CHAPTER 3

FAMILY, COMMUNITY, AND POLITICS, 1933–1939

◇ ◇ ◇

A variety of factors shaped the experiences of African Americans during the Great Depression. The impact of economic hard times, the emergence of New Deal social programs, and changing perspectives on race and class helped to define the black experience. Despite widespread deprivation and suffering, African Americans developed strategies for coping with the depression on their own. They deepened their connections with family, friends, and the African-American community. At the same time, they strengthened their links with organized labor and broadened their participation in the political process, particularly the New Deal coalition of the Democratic party. As early as 1932, Robert Vann, editor of the black weekly newspaper the *Pittsburgh Courier,* had urged African Americans to abandon the party of Lincoln. "My friends, go turn Lincoln's picture to the wall. That debt has been paid in full."

As the depression took its toll on their lives, African Americans developed new ways to make ends meet. For many black women the depression was an old experience with a new name. As black men lost jobs in increasing numbers, African-American women helped keep their families intact by relying on black kin and friendship networks. As the novelist Richard Wright put it in an essay on the period, "There is nothing—no ownership or lust for power—that stands between us and our kin. And we reckon kin not as others do, but down to the ninth and tenth cousin. And for a reason we cannot explain we are mighty proud when we

African Americans meet at a YMCA in Pittsburgh in 1938 for a "Youth Conference for Vocational Opportunity" sponsored by the National Youth Administration, a New Deal agency, and the National Urban League.

The wife and daughter of a government employee can food with the help of a pressure cooker in 1939. Canning food, planting vegetable gardens, fishing, and hunting helped black families to survive during the depression.

meet a man, woman, or child who, in talking to us, reveals that the blood of our brood has somehow entered his veins."

African-American families took in boarders, cared for each other's children, and creatively manipulated their resources. In rural areas, they maintained gardens, canned fruits and vegetables, fished, hunted, and gathered wild nuts and berries. A Georgia relief official understood these creative responses to poverty: "There is no dearth of resourcefulness. In their efforts to maintain existence, these people are catching and selling fish, reselling vegetables, sewing in exchange for old clothes, letting out sleeping space, and doing odd jobs. They understand how to help each other. Stoves are used in common, wash boilers go their rounds, and garden crops are exchanged and shared." African Americans also adapted these rural responses to the realities of life in cities. In small urban spaces, for example, some blacks planted gardens to supply certain southern staples, particularly collard greens, cabbage, potatoes, and tomatoes. Under the impact of the depression, such activities became even more important.

Since the threat of eviction weighed so heavily on the minds of urban blacks, the "rent party" represented a significant source of income. Sometimes described as "chitlins struts," these parties had deep roots in the rural South. "Down home" food—chitlins, corn bread, collard greens, hogmaws, pig feet, and so on—was on the menu. Sponsors charged a small admission fee and sometimes offered printed or handwritten tickets with rhymes to capture the spiritual or cultural dimensions of the event.

Shake it, break it, hang it on the wall
Sling it out the window and catch it before it falls.
Save your tears for a rainy day
We are giving a party where you can play
With red mammas and too bad Sheabas
Who wear their dresses above their knees
And mess around with whom they please.

Street musicians in Harlem in 1943. The hard times brought on by the depression provided inspiration to a generation of black blues artists.

A key component in the survival of urban blacks during the 1930s, rent parties also served as a training ground for the next generation of black blues artists—the blues men. As the commercial recording studios recovered from the depression, they helped to spread the music of the urban black blues men who followed in the wake of such classical blues recording artists as Bessie Smith, LeRoy Carr, Jimmy Yancey, Cripple Clarence Lofton, Big Maceo Merriweather, Sonny Boy Williamson, and Big Bill Broonzy, among others moved to the fore with lyrics familiar to the house parties.

> How Long, how long has that evening train been gone
> How long, how long, baby, how long?
> Standing at the station, watch my baby leaving town
> Feeling disgusted, nowhere could she be found.
> How long, how long, baby, how long?

Such parties became even more lucrative when sponsors added gambling and liquor to food, music, and dancing. The "policy" or numbers game was also an adaptation to poverty that African Americans brought to the city and used to help weather the storm during the Great Depression. The game had its roots in the mid-19th century, but it gained increasing popularity among the poor, because it permitted bets of as low as a penny. On the South Side of Chicago, one black resident tried to imagine a world without policy. It was so important to Chicago's black community that without it, he believed, "7,000 people would be unemployed and business in general would be crippled, especially taverns and even groceries, shoestores, and many other business enterprises who depend on the buying power of the South Side."

The church provided another arena in which African Americans sought to make ends meet. Established Baptist, Methodist, and Holiness (Church of God in Christ) churches struggled to assist their parishioners to survive hard times. New religious movements also increased their following, partly as a result of their success in feeding their parishioners. For example, the Peace Mission movement of Father Divine (George Baker), whose efforts on behalf of the unemployed started during the 1920s, expanded dramatically during the depression. In 1932, he moved the mission from New Jersey to Harlem and gained credit for feeding the masses and offering hope in a time of widespread despair.

At the same time, Bishop Charles Emmanuel Grace, known as "Daddy Grace," established the United House of Prayer of All People,

The pastor of the Church of God in Christ in Washington, D.C., preaches during a service in 1942. Black churches also featured music that mirrored the growing influence of urban life.

with headquarters in Washington, D.C. The organization spread to more than 20 cities and provided thousands of people respite from hard times. Sometimes religious institutions took on the character of the "rent party." In Milwaukee, for example, a Holiness minister and his wife held services in their home, as their daughter recalled: "My mother's home was always open to all strangers. . . . When my father would be at work, these people would come to the home, . . . and she really pushed, when my father would come home, she would have a house full, we would go from home to home, and sing and pray and administer the word of God. We'd wash dirty clothes. We'd take food and feed them, and every day every evening, we'd bring like 6, 7, 8 souls into God."

Black religious services also featured music that sometimes re- sembled the music of the "rent party." It was in 1932 that the gospel pioneer Thomas Dorsey broke from his growing reputation as a blues pianist and dedicated himself to gospel song writing, which led to his most popular tune, "Precious Lord." Dorsey's swinging, rocking rhythms and blueslike melodies eventually caught on and stirred the entire world. Over and over again, whether in religious or secular settings, black children of the depression recalled how their families struggled to place food on the tables and clothes on their backs.

In order to improve the circumstances of their families and communities, African Americans also moved increasingly toward the labor movement, which had grown enormously under the impact of New Deal legislation. The new Congress of Industrial Organizations (CIO) increasingly displaced the older, more racially restrictive American Federation of Labor (AFL). Under these new conditions, African Americans took the initiative to expand their place within labor's ranks. In Milwaukee, for example, LeRoy Johnson, a black butcher and packinghouse worker, became a major figure in the organization of the local United Packinghouse Union. Described by an associate as an "aggressive sort of guy and quite articulate," Johnson helped make the CIO campaign in the city a success.

Perhaps more than any other single figure during the 1930s, however, A. Philip Randolph epitomized the persistent effort of black workers to organize in their own interest. Born in Crescent City, Florida, in 1889, Randolph was the son of an African Methodist Episcopal minister and an equally hard-working and productive mother. He migrated to New York in 1911. During World War I he copublished the antiwar socialist magazine *The Messenger* and was soon denounced by the U.S. attorney general as "the most dangerous Negro in America." In 1925, he

By organizing the Brotherhood of Sleeping Car Porters, a union that represented almost 35,000 black Pullman porters, A. Philip Randolph brought blacks a much greater voice in shaping national labor policy.

spearheaded the formation of the Brotherhood of Sleeping Car Porters (and Maids) (BSCP), a black union, which the AFL refused to recognize. During the 1930s, however, when new federal legislation (the Railway Labor Act of 1934) recognized the rights of workers to organize, Randolph and the BSCP increased their organizing drive among black porters. Randolph's rhetoric and actions inspired the rank and file during the hard days of the depression. At one convention, he exclaimed, "The lesson that Pullman porters in particular and Negroes in general must learn is that salvation must and can only come from within." Another officer, Ashley Totten, reinforced Randolph's inspiring words, adding, "When the U.S. finished the War of Revolution the people were ragged, the wives and children were barefoot, the homes had not even window panes to keep out the cold; but America had her independence just the same."

Black Pullman porters rallied to the BSCP. By 1933 the union claimed to represent some 35,000 members. Two years later the BSCP defeated a Pullman Company union and gained the right to represent porters in negotiations with management, which, in 1937, signed a contract with the union. In the meantime, the AFL had grudgingly approved a full international charter for the brotherhood, placing it on an equal footing with other member unions. The BSCP victory had extraordinary significance: It not only helped to make blacks more union conscious, but allowed them to have greater influence on national labor policy and the larger civil rights struggle.

As black workers increased their organizing activities, the major civil rights organizations also moved toward a sharper focus on the economic plight of African Americans. In 1933 the NAACP, the Urban League, and other interracial organizations formed the Joint Committee on National Recovery (JCNR). Although underfunded and ill staffed, the JCNR lobbied in Washington, D.C., on behalf of blacks and helped to publicize the plight of African Americans in the relief and recovery programs. The Urban League also formed emergency advisory councils and Negro workers' councils in large cities across the country and played a major role in promoting closer ties between blacks and organized labor. Although the league had earlier supported black strikebreaking activities and emphasized amicable relations with employers, it now urged black workers to organize and "get into somebody's union and stay there." For

The New York chapter of the Brotherhood of Sleeping Car Porters lines up for a 1936 parade to celebrate the 11th anniversary of its founding.

its part, the NAACP formed a group called the Committee on Economic Problems Affecting the Negro; invited representatives of the CIO to serve on its board; and worked with organized labor to gain housing, wages, hours, and Social Security benefits for black workers.

The major civil rights organizations also supported the "Don't Buy Where You Can't Work" campaign. Aimed at white merchants who served the African-American community but refused to employ blacks, "Don't Buy Where You Can't Work" galvanized the black urban community. In New York, Chicago, Washington, D.C., and other cities, blacks boycotted stores that refused to hire them, or hired them only as low-paying domestic and common laborers.

New York launched its "Don't Buy Where You Can't Work" campaign under the leadership of Reverend John H. Johnson of St. Martin's Protestant Episcopal Church. When white Harlem store owners refused to negotiate, Johnson and his supporters formed the Citizens League for

Fair Play, which set up picket lines around Blumstein's Department Store, took pictures of blacks who crossed the line, and published the photos in a black newspaper, the *New York Age*. After six weeks, the store gave in and hired black clerical and professional staff. As a result of such actions, New York blacks obtained the nation's first black affirmative action plan—a pattern of hiring that gave preference to previously excluded groups. In 1938 the New York Uptown Chamber of Commerce negotiated with the Greater New York Coordinating Committee for Employment and agreed to grant African Americans one-third of all retail executive, clerical, and sales jobs. The businesses would not fire whites to make room for blacks, but agreed to give blacks preference in filling all new openings.

Although African Americans expressed their resentment to discrimination in formally organized and peaceful group actions, they sometimes despaired and adopted violent responses. On March 25, 1935, a race riot broke out in Harlem when a rumor spread that a black youth had been brutally beaten and nearly killed by the police. Flyers soon appeared: "Child Brutally Beaten—near death," "One Hour Ago Negro Boy Was Brutally Beaten," "The Boy Is Near Death." Although the youth in question had been released unharmed, outrage had already spread and African Americans smashed buildings and looted stores in a night of violence that resulted in at least one death, more than 50 injuries, and thousands of dollars' worth of property damage. In his novel *Invisible Man*, Ralph Ellison later described the event:

> I could see a crowd rushing a store . . . moving in, and a fusillade of canned goods, salami, liverwurst, hogs heads and chitterlings belching out to those outside . . . as now out of the dark of the intersecting street two mounted policemen came at a gallop . . . charging straight into the swarming mass. They came toward me as I ran, a crowd of men and women carrying cases of beer, cheese, chains of linked sausage, watermelons, sacks of sugar, hams, cornmeal, fuel lamps.

In the volatile climate of the 1930s, some blacks gravitated toward the Communist and Socialist parties. They perceived radicalism as the most appropriate response to the deepening plight of African Americans. In 1931, aided by the Communist party, blacks in rural Alabama founded the Alabama Sharecroppers Union. The organization developed an underground network of communications that enabled it to maintain

secrecy. Meetings took place in black churches, where their plans were disguised as religious undertakings. The union's membership increased to an estimated 3,000 in 1934. Its efforts soon attracted the attention of local authorities and violence broke out when law officers tried to confiscate the livestock of union members who allegedly owed money to landowners. In 1932, Ned Cobb (who was renamed Nate Shaw in the published oral history of his life) joined the sharecroppers union and fought the system that oppressed him. As he recalled, he had to act because he had labored "under many rulins, just like the other Negro, that I knowed was injurious to man and displeasin to God and still I had to fall back." One cold morning in December 1932, Shaw refused to "fall back." When deputy sheriffs came to seize his neighbor's livestock, he took part in a shootout with local law officers. He reported that before he could reach for his gun, the law officers

Black women typists in a Pittsburgh office in 1939. Boycotts in New York, Chicago, and other cities against businesses that refused to offer blacks clerical or sales jobs opened the doors for these women and many others.

filled my hind end up from the bend of my legs to my hips with shot. I
walked on in the door, stopped right in the hallway and looked back. He [a
law officer] was standin right close to a big old oak tree right in line with the
door. Run my hand in my pocket, snatched out my .32 Smith and Wesson
and I commenced a shooting at Platt. Good God he jumped behind that tree
soon as that pistol fired; he jumped like lightnin. My mind told me: just keep
shooting the tree, just keep shootin and maybe he'll get scared and run;
you'll have a chance at him then. But as the devil would have it, the more I
shot the tighter he drawed up behind that tree until I quit shootin. I seed his
head poke around the tree—that tree saved him—and he seed what I was
doin: good God almighty, I was reloadin and before I could reload my gun . . .
[e]very one of them officers [4 in all] outrun the devil away from there. I
don't know how many people they might have thought was in that house, but
that .32 Smith and Wesson was barkin too much for 'em to stand. They didn't
see where the shots was comin from—nobody but Mr. Platt knowed that.

Nate Shaw's action underscored the increasing militancy of rural
black workers. Despite violence and intimidation, black workers also
took an active part in the formation of the socialist Southern Tenant
Farmers Union (STFU). A black farmer helped to inspire the organization when he spoke up at the initial meeting of the group: "For a long
time now the white folks and the colored folks have been fighting each
other and both of us has been getting whipped all the time. We don't
have nothing against one another but we got plenty against the landlord.
The same chain that holds my people holds your people too. If we're
chained together on the outside, ought to stay chained together in the
union." When white landowners evicted sharecroppers in Arkansas, the
black vice president of the STFU, Owen H. Whitfield, led some 500
black and white farmers onto the main highway between Memphis and
St. Louis and vowed to remain there until the federal government inter-
vened. The Missouri State Highway Patrol soon moved in and loaded
families and their possessions on trucks and scattered them on back
country roads. Although these radical actions produced few results, they
highlighted the increasing activism of rural black workers in their own
behalf.

A small number of blacks joined the Communist party and played a
role in the party's League of Struggle for Negro Rights (LSNR). According to a recent study of the party in depression-era Alabama, blacks made
up the majority of the party's membership during most of the period.

The party's fight on behalf of the Scottsboro Boys attracted local black steelworkers such as Al Murphy and Hosea Hudson. Al Murphy was born in McRae, Georgia, in 1908, grew up in a poor sharecropping family, and moved to Birmingham, Alabama, in 1923. In Birmingham, he worked as a common laborer and attended night school. Unfortunately, as he recalled, during the depression "I had to stop night school and join workers on breadlines." Shortly thereafter, he attended a Communist party meeting for the unemployed. Impressed by what he saw and heard, he joined the party that same night, dedicated himself to party work, and soon recruited other black steelworkers for membership.

Born in a sharecropping family in Wilkes County, Georgia, in 1898, Hosea Hudson was among those that Al Murphy recruited. As a youngster, Hudson worked hard on the land. He moved to Birmingham in 1923

At a makeshift campsite by the side of a highway, these evicted sharecroppers in New Madrid County, Missouri, ponder their next move.

and gained employment as an iron molder at a local foundry. Hudson later recalled that he always "resented injustice" and the way whites treated blacks. After failing to organize black workers independently and witnessing the Communist campaign to free the Scottsboro Boys, Hudson joined the Communist party in September 1931. He later recalled the sorts of injustice that led him to the party: "Blacks are the last to be hired and the first to be fired. It was we, already existing on the crumbling edge of starvation, who suffered the highest death rate. If we had any medical care at all, it was just a whisper above being nothing." During the struggle to free Communist party member Angelo Herndon, Herndon's black defense attorney, Benjamin Davis, Jr., also joined the party. A graduate of Amherst College and Harvard Law School, Davis later explained his decision as "the only rational and realistic path to the freedom which burns in the breast of every Negro. It required only a moment to join but my whole lifetime as a Negro American prepared me for the moment."

Most African Americans shunned membership in radical parties and worked hard to broaden their participation in the New Deal coalition. In 1936 African Americans formed the National Negro Congress (NNC). Spearheaded by Ralph Bunche, professor of political science at Howard University, and John Davis, executive secretary of the Joint Committee on National Recovery, the organization aimed to unite all existing black organizations—political, fraternal, and religious—and press for the full socioeconomic recovery of the black community from the ravages of the depression. Representatives of nearly 600 organizations attended the founding meeting, which selected A. Philip Randolph as its first president.

The National Negro Congress demonstrated a new level of African-American political organization and mobilization. Because of the dramatic growth of the black population in most large cities, black voter registration drives picked up momentum during the 1930s. The proportion of the black population that had registered to vote had risen rapidly in the major industrial cities—from less than 30 percent to 66 percent in Detroit. In Philadelphia the number of registered black voters rose by more than 90 percent. In Chicago the rate of black voter registration exceeded the percentage of white. In the South as well—Durham, Raleigh, Birmingham, Atlanta, Savannah, and Charleston—African Americans formed political clubs to fight for the franchise and increase the number of black voters in that region.

As Republicans continued to ignore the pleas of black voters, blacks increasingly turned toward the Democratic party. In the election of 1936, African Americans had voted for the Democratic party in record numbers, giving Roosevelt 76 percent of the northern black vote. Following that election, African Americans used their growing support of the Democratic party to demand greater consideration from federal policymakers.

African Americans placed justice before the law high on their list of priorities. In 1933 the NAACP organized a Writers League Against Lynching and launched a nationwide movement to secure a federal antilynching law. Sponsored in the House of Representatives by Edward Costigan of Colorado and in the Senate by Robert Wagner of New York, the antilynching bill gained little support from FDR and failed when southern senators killed the measure in 1934, 1935, 1937, 1938, and 1940. Despite its failure, the campaign against lynching produced results. The number of lynchings nationwide dropped from 18 in 1935 to 2 in 1939. Under the leadership of the black attorneys William Hastie, Charles Hamilton Houston, and Thurgood Marshall, African Americans won important cases before the U.S. Supreme Court: selection of blacks for jury duty; admission to previously all-white law schools; and greater access to employment, housing, and public accommodations. Houston, Marshall, and Hastie carefully planned an overall strategy, emphasizing test cases with broad implications for dismantling the entire segregationist system.

Missouri ex rel. Gaines v. *Canada* (1938) was one of the most celebrated of these cases. Houston's decision to take the case represented a

A. Philip Randolph delivers the presidential address at the Second National Negro Congress in 1937. In his speech Randolph said that the Second NNC "comes at a crucial period of transition in the life of the world and the Negro race. . . . The Negro people are . . . becoming more conscious of their rights as American citizens."

tactical maneuver to dismantle the separate but equal principle which the Court established in an earlier case, *Plessy* v. *Ferguson* (1896). Lloyd Gaines, a black graduate of Lincoln University in Missouri, was denied admission to the University of Missouri Law School because the school did not accept blacks. The university advised Gaines to take advantage of state funds provided to support black legal training in other states. Supported by the St. Louis chapter of the NAACP, Gaines sued, demanding access to training at the all-white law school. Houston argued the case in the Missouri courts, where Gaines lost. Then Houston took the case to the U.S. Supreme Court, where Gaines won a major victory. The Court's decision outlawed the practice of giving blacks subsidies to receive legal training at out-of-state schools. It also supported the admission of blacks to all-white schools in the absence of fully equal facilities for blacks.

As the number of blacks living in major cities increased during the 1930s, black political and community organizations encouraged the newcomers to register to vote. Here, blacks line up to register in Atlanta.

A twin lynching in Marian, Indiana, on August 8, 1930. The Ku Klux Klan had moved to the urban North and West during the 1920s and gained its greatest influence in Indiana.

As black lawyers attacked the legal foundations of Jim Crow, as the system of legalized racial segregation was called, black social scientists and artists assaulted its intellectual underpinnings. E. Franklin Frazier, W. E. B. Du Bois, Carter G. Woodson, and other black social scientists and historians had worked for years counteracting racist stereotypes. Under the leadership of Woodson, the Association for the Study of Negro Life and History (founded in 1915) continued to promote the study of African-American history, emphasizing the contributions of blacks to the development of the nation. While the organization continued to publish the scholarly *Journal of Negro History* (founded in 1916), in 1933 it added the *Negro History Bulletin* as a publication designed for broader circulation. Launched in 1926, Negro History Week, featuring lectures and discussions on the black experience, also became a regular part of African-American community life across the country.

E. Franklin Frazier conducted important early studies of black community and family life, which culminated in the publication of his book *The Negro Family in the United States* in 1939. Although he underestimated the role that poor and working-class blacks played in shaping their own experience, Frazier emphasized environmental over racial factors in explaining poverty. In his scholarship on African-American history, W. E. B. Du Bois also called attention to the impact of class and racial discrimination in his massive reinterpretation of the emancipation period, *Black Reconstruction in America, 1860–1880,* published in 1935. Gunnar Myrdal's *An American Dilemma* (1944) built upon the scholarship of some 30 black scholars, including young men like Charles S. Johnson, St. Clair Drake, Horace R. Cayton, and Ralph Bunche.

Reinforcing the work of black social scientists and historians were the contributions of black artists. The concert singers Roland Hayes, Raul Robeson, Dorothy Maynor, and Marian Anderson frequently appeared on stage and on national radio broadcasts.

Born in to a working-class family in Philadelphia in 1902, Marian Anderson had pursued advanced musical training in Europe and had performed widely in the Scandinavian countries of Sweden, Norway, and Denmark. Following one concert, the internationally renowned conductor Arturo Toscanini exclaimed: "What I heard today one is privileged to hear only once in a hundred years." As a result of her growing success in Europe, Anderson returned to the United States in 1935. *The New York*

Times reported, "Marian Anderson has returned to her native land one of the great singers of our time."

In 1939 the Daughters of the American Revolution, who owned Constitution Hall in Washington, D.C., barred Anderson from giving a concert there. For her part, Eleanor Roosevelt resigned from the DAR over the incident. In her popular newspaper column, "My Day," she explained that she could no longer belong to an organization that maintained the color line. African Americans and their white allies formed a committee of protest and got permission from Secretary of the Interior Harold Ickes to hold the concert at the Lincoln Memorial. Nearly 75,000 people stood in the cold open air to hear her sing, and millions more heard her on radio. Her repertoire included Negro spirituals, bringing them to a wide audience for the first time, along with the works of classic European "art music" composers.

Richard Wright, Langston Hughes, William Attaway, and others expressed the experiences of African Americans through novels and plays. In 1938, Richard Wright won a WPA writing prize for his book *Uncle Tom's Children,* a collection of short stories on black life in the rural

With the launch of Negro History Week in 1926 blacks were encouraged to look back with pride on the contributions of their ancestors to the development of the United States. These teachers in Missouri display material that they can use in their classrooms to give their students a fuller picture of the black experience.

After Marian Anderson was barred by the DAR from performing in Constitution Hall in Washington, D.C., she gave a concert on the steps of the Lincoln Memorial. Tens of thousands of people stood outside in the cold and millions more listened on the radio to her historic concert.

South. Two years later he published his most famous novel, *Native Son,* which chronicled the great migration of blacks to American cities and the destructive impact of racism on their lives. One observer later recalled that "the day *Native Son* appeared, American culture was changed forever." Wright's book was a phenomenal success. It set a sales record for Harper and Brothers and soon surpassed John Steinbeck's *The Grapes of Wrath* on the best-seller lists. Born on a plantation near Natchez, Mississippi, in 1908, Wright later wrote that his head was "full of a hazy notion that life could be lived with dignity, that the personalities of others should not be violated." The Mississippi-born writer William Attaway expressed similar sentiments in his powerful portrayal of black steelworkers in his novel *Blood on the Forge* (1941).

Adding to the artistic portrayal of black life were the dramatic productions of black theater groups such as the Rose McClendon Players, the Harlem Players, and the Negro People's Theatre; the music of jazz artists such as Fletcher Henderson, Duke Ellington, Bessie Smith, and Jimmie Lunceford; the paintings of Romare Bearden; and the films of the pioneer black filmmaker Oscar Micheaux. African Americans also gained greater access to mainstream radio and film and gradually used these media to project more positive images of themselves than previously was possible. The blues singer Ethel Waters had her own radio show, and the film industry broke new ground by giving Paul Robeson the lead role in the movie version of the stage play *The Emperor Jones,* with whites serving as supporting cast.

African Americans developed a variety of responses to life during the Great Depression. The depression presented different problems and

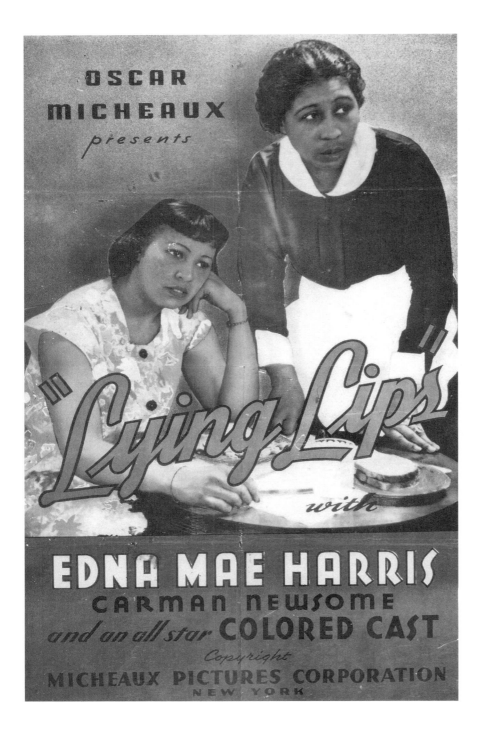

Lying Lips, *a 1939 movie produced and directed by the pioneering black filmmaker Oscar Micheaux, featured an all-black cast.*

offered different prospects for educated black professional people on the one hand and the masses of working-class and poor people on the other. Yet all were linked to each other through the persistence of racial inequality, which limited the opportunities of African Americans across class, generational, and gender lines. The emergence of prizefighter Joe Louis as a folk hero for all African Americans is perhaps the most potent evidence of their sense of a common plight, kinship, and future. Indeed, Louis helped to unify black people during the period and gave them hope that they could topple the segregationist system. When he lost they cried, as in his first bout against the German fighter Max Schmeling in 1936. They were especially heartbroken because Hitler preached the doctrine of Aryan supremacy, which claimed the physical and intellectual superiority of all white people, and the German people in particular. As Maya Angelou recalls in her book *I Know Why the Caged Bird Sings:* "It was our people falling. It was another lynching, yet another Black man hanging on a tree. One more woman ambushed and raped. A Black boy whipped and maimed. It was hounds on the trail of a man running through slimy swamps. It was a white woman slapping her maid for being forgetful."

On the other hand, when Joe Louis won, black people celebrated. After he knocked out Max Schmeling in the first round of their rematch, black people everywhere applauded, celebrated, and danced in the streets. Similarly, when Louis knocked out the Italian heavyweight Primo Carnera, black people were also elated and felt that they had to some degree avenged Benito Mussolini's invasion and bombing of Ethiopia in 1935. Following Louis's fight with another opponent, black children created a rhyme that they sung as they bounced balls and jumped rope: "I went down town last Tuesday night/To see Joe Louis and Max Baer fight/When Joe Louis socked, Max Baer rocked." The singer Lena Horne offers a powerful statement on Louis's role as a black folk hero: "Joe was the one invincible Negro, the one who stood up to the white man and beat him down with his fists. He in a sense carried so many of our hopes, maybe even dreams of vengeance."

The depression, New Deal, and social change sent a mixed message to African Americans. On the one hand, they experienced the gradual growth of new and more egalitarian ideas and practices on race; on the other, they suffered persistent economic deprivation and discrimination.

Because of this dual process of poverty and progress, African-American responses were likewise complex and varied. At times, they despaired and exploded into violence, as in the Harlem riot of 1935. At other times, they gave up on mainstream institutions and turned toward alternative visions and strategies, as reflected in their growing connections with the

Jazz great Duke Ellington on stage at the Hurricane Club in New York City, May 1943.

Heavyweight Joe Louis in the ring against German fighter Max Schmeling in 1938. After Louis's victory, black people everywhere spilled into the streets to dance and celebrate.

Communist and Socialist parties. Their music also reflected a similar range of responses—blues, gospel, and jazz. Above all, however, as symbolized in the boxing career of Joe Louis, they deepened their struggle to break down barriers to their full participation in American society. They launched movements to break the back of Jim Crow and broaden their access to the larger economic, political, social, and cultural life of the nation. Their struggle would bear even greater fruit during the crisis of World War II, another epic fight that lay only a few years ahead.

CHAPTER 4
WORLD WAR II, 1940–1945
◇ ◇ ◇

U nder the impact of World War II, African Americans gained new industrial opportunities as the nation mobilized for war and called men into the military in rising numbers. It was during this period that African Americans regained a foothold in the industrial economy and broke through the unskilled "job ceiling" to move into semiskilled and skilled jobs. Yet the movement of African Americans into defense industry jobs was a slow process. Employers, labor unions, and government agencies still discriminated against blacks and undermined their participation in the war effort. The *Chicago Defender,* a black weekly, captured the frustrations of many African Americans in an editorial. "Why die for democracy for some foreign country when we don't even have it here? . . . What Democracy have we enjoyed since the last World War? Are our people segregated? Are they not Jim-Crowed and lynched? Are their civil and constitutional rights respected?"

Most African Americans nonetheless supported the nation's declarations of war against Germany and Japan. Black servicemen and women fought in the European, Pacific, and Mediterranean theaters of war. But in contrast to their attitudes during World War I, African Americans refused to simply "close ranks" and postpone their own struggle for full citizenship and recognition of their rights at home. They now used the war emergency, as well as their growing influence in the Democratic party and the new unions, to wage a "Double V" campaign—for victory at home as well as abroad. Their campaign received its most powerful

Members of the 41st Engineers on parade at Fort Bragg, North Carolina, during World War II. The Office of War Information used this photograph in its promotional booklet "Negroes and the War."

Blacks continued to struggle against racial discrimination at home, even as African-American soldiers fought and died overseas during World War II.

expression in the militant March on Washington, which led to the federal Fair Employment Practices Committee. By war's end African Americans and their white allies had set the stage for the emergence of the modern civil rights movement.

As the nation edged toward war in the years after 1939, African Americans continued to face a pattern of racial discrimination. Despite growing U.S. protests against the racism of Nazi Germany, African Americans confronted racial injustice at home and abroad. In the defense industries and armed services, African Americans complained of racial bias. In 1940 blacks made up less than 2 percent of employees in the nation's expanding aircraft industry, and management officials in that industry often stated overtly their determination to keep blacks out. At the large North American Aviation firm, for example, the company's president reported that black applicants would be considered only for janitorial jobs: "We will receive applications from both white and Negro workers. However, the Negroes will be considered only as janitors and in other similar capacities. . . . While we are in complete sympathy with the Negro, it is against the company policy to employ them as mechanics or aircraft workers. We use none except white workers in the plant . . . at Inglewood [California] and the plant in Dallas and we intend to maintain the same policy in Kansas City." When black workers did seek employment on all-white jobs, they endured a series of humiliating responses from employers. Some companies informed black workers that they only hired white men. Other firms discouraged blacks even more directly. In Milwaukee, the A. O. Smith Company, producer of auto frames and tanks for the military, stated that they "never did and didn't intend to employ Negroes." Black women confronted even greater difficulties gaining defense jobs than black men did. Employers expressed the belief that black women were peculiarly suited for domestic service but not for industrial jobs. When black women applied for war industry jobs, some employers told them that "my wife needs a maid." Others said that their plants lacked segregated bathrooms for black and white women. Still others justified the exclusion of black women on the basis of maintaining harmony in the all-white workplace. In Detroit, for example, a personnel manager in a bomber plant remarked that "when a department is nice and peaceful [we] don't go around looking for trouble by putting colored people in the department." Thus many African-American men and

women believed that it was a waste of time to seek work in all-white defense plants.

Craft unions reinforced discrimination against black workers in defense work. Skilled black workers—plumbers, bricklayers, carpenters, electricians, cement finishers, and painters—faced exclusion from labor unions either by provisions of their bylaws or by some form of "ritual," or gentleman's agreement that blacks would not be proposed for membership. In a resolution introduced at the 1941 convention of the AFL, the black labor leader A. Philip Randolph pinpointed labor union discrimination against black workers in a broad range of jobs in different parts of the country:

> Negro painters in Omaha cannot get into the painter's organization nor can they secure a charter. Plasterers and cement finishers in Kansas City, Missouri, cannot get into the organization nor can they get a charter. The A. F. of L. unions in shipbuilding yards in New Orleans refuse membership to Negro workers, although the company has expressed a willingness to employ them. . . . In St. Louis, Negro artisans cannot get work, but white workers come from outside St. Louis and are sent to work.

The SS Frederick Douglass *was built by an integrated work force at the Bethlehem-Fairfield shipyard in Baltimore.*

Randolph cited the International Association of Machinists (IAM) as the union with the most conspicuous record of labor union discrimination against African Americans. By accepting only white members, the IAM reinforced the exclusion of blacks from the metal trades and the aircraft industry, including the huge Boeing Aircraft Corporation in Seattle.

Since many defense industry jobs required additional training for large numbers of white as well as black workers, the U.S. Office of Education financed such programs under the Vocational Education National Defense (VEND) Training Program. In his study of black labor during the period, the economist and New Deal official Robert Weaver documented racial discrimination in such programs. According to Weaver, this kind of discrimination had deep roots in earlier patterns of discrimination in federal educational programs. During the 1930s, the federal government had already established a precedent for discrimination by awarding blacks less than $4.75 per capita (that is, per person, on average) of federal funds, compared to $8 for whites. When the government established VEND, it continued the same practices. As Weaver put it, "This discrimination was in reality a projection of past practices. Most

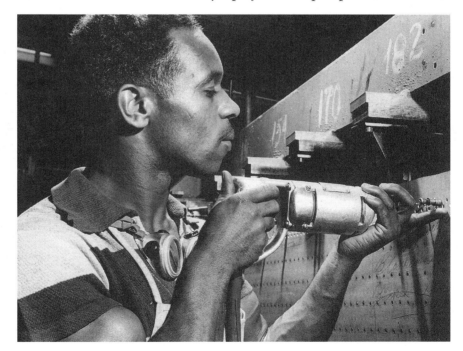

An African-American worker uses a portable electric drill at a western aircraft plant. With the start of World War II, the defense industry scrambled to find and train workers.

vocational education officials at the national, state, and local levels were not prepared to champion new policies relative to minority groups' training." Vocational training programs reinforced a vicious cycle of black exclusion from defense jobs. When asked why blacks were not trained and employed in the defense industry, training school supervisors, unions, and employers conveniently blamed each other, thus passing the buck back and forth and assuring that nothing was done about their discriminatory practices.

African Americans fared little better in the armed services. During the early 1940s, as the government trained white pilots to fly warplanes, the War Department barred African Americans from the U.S. Air Corps. Blacks were admitted to the U.S. Army in large numbers, but were placed in segregated service and labor units, responsible for building, maintenance, and supplies. In 1940 there were an estimated 5,000 blacks in the army, but only four black units were up to full strength, and there were fewer than 12 black officers in a corps of more than 230,000

Protesters outside the Democratic National Convention in 1940 carry signs calling for an end to discrimination in the armed services.

Black seamen aboard a Coast Guard patrol vessel watch for German submarines in the Atlantic. At the start of the war, blacks had been barred from serving in the Coast Guard, except as laborers and housekeepers.

enlisted men and officers. At the war's outset, the Marine Corps and Air Corps barred blacks completely, while the Department of the Navy and the Coast Guard accepted them only as messmen or laborers. Rear Admiral Chester W. Nimitz defended the navy's position, emphasizing the need for efficiency: "After many years of experience, the policy of not enlisting men of color for any branch of the naval service except the messmen's branch was adopted to meet the best interests of general ship efficiency." Blacks who did volunteer often received a hostile reception, particularly in the South. In many cases they were told that "Negroes aren't wanted." In Charlotte, North Carolina, recruiting officers informed blacks that the recruiting station itself was for "whites only."

Despite the existence of racial discrimination in the defense program, African Americans played a key role in the war effort. The number of blacks selected for military service increased from 2,069 in 1940 to about 370,000 in 1942, following the Japanese attack on Pearl Harbor on December 7, 1941, and the official entry of the United States into World

忠
魂
碑

A group of Marines rests at the base of a Japanese war memorial on the island of Okinawa, the site of some of the fiercest fighting during the war. Black troops were among the first to go ashore.

War II. By the end of the war, nearly 1 million black men and women had served in the armed forces, nearly three-quarters in the U.S. Army, followed in numbers by service in the navy (and Coast Guard), Marine Corps, and the Air Corps, in which only a few blacks served. At the same time, black civilians supported the war effort by purchasing war bonds through vigorous bond campaigns in their churches, schools, and community organizations. Despite the poverty of many, they also cooperated with the government's food conservation program and staffed United

Service Organization (USO) posts to boost the morale of black service men and women. The USO coordinated the social service activities of a wide range of organizations, including the YWCA, YMCA, and the Salvation Army, to name a few. In addition, African Americans served as nurses' aides, drivers in motor corps, and other voluntary but vital jobs in the Red Cross.

Nearly 500,000 African Americans saw service overseas. Most served in transportation corps, port battalions, and construction units. They moved troops and supplies, built and repaired roads and fortifications, and cleared battle zones of debris and dead and wounded soldiers. They also engaged the enemy in combat in the European, Mediterranean, and Pacific theaters, and gained recognition for their outstanding services. The 761st Tank Battalion, which served in six European countries and fought in the Battle of the Bulge, received several commendations for its bravery on the battlefield. By war's end, many of these units received the Presidential Citation for their contributions to winning the war. Several African Americans received the Navy Cross. Messman Dorie Miller became perhaps the most renowned of these seamen. "Without previous experience," read the citation, "[he] manned a machine gun in the face of serious fire during the Japanese attack on Pearl

First Lieutenant Lee Rayford served with the all-black 99th Fighter Squadron in Italy. At the outbreak of World War II, blacks had been barred from serving in the Air Corps, yet by the end of the war 82 black pilots had received the Distinguished Flying Cross.

Harbor, December 7, 1941, on the Battleship *Arizona* shooting down four enemy planes."

The Air Corps awarded the Distinguished Flying Cross to 82 African-American pilots. This achievement was made possible by the training of black airmen at segregated institutions, like Tuskegee Institute. Although some black leaders resisted the training of blacks in segregated facilities, others accepted the arrangement as an opportunity to expand their war- and peace-time opportunities. Tuskegee trained some 600 black pilots, who flew missions in Africa, France, Italy, Poland, Romania, and Germany. Colonel Benjamin O. Davis, a graduate of the U.S. Military Academy at West Point, became the highest ranking black officer. He flew 60 missions and won several medals for distinguished service. According to one of his citations, Davis

> led his group on a penetration escort attack in the Munich area June 9, 1944. The bomber formation was attacked by more than one hundred enemy fighters near Udine, Italy. Faced with the problem of protecting the large bomber formation with the comparatively few fighters under his control, Colonel Davis so skillfully disposed of his squadron that in spite of the large number of enemy fighters, the bomber formation suffered only a few losses.

Cadets in the U.S. Army's first all-black air unit, the 99th Pursuit Squadron, were trained at Tuskegee Institute in Alabama. More than 600 black pilots were trained there during the war.

African-American women service a truck at Fort Huachuca, Arizona. During the war, black women, perhaps even more so than white women, performed traditionally male jobs.

Other African Americans received medals of honor from the governments of France, Yugoslavia, and the Soviet Union.

African Americans served and achieved against great odds. On and off military bases, black service personnel often did not receive courteous treatment and recognition of their human and civil rights. In Durham, North Carolina, for example, a local jury acquitted a white bus driver who murdered a black soldier following an altercation on his route. When German prisoners of war arrived in the United States, they often received service in white establishments that denied service to African Americans. En route to prison camps, many southern white communities served German prisoners while denying food, toilets, and other necessities to blacks. Moreover, once in prison camps, the prevailing system of segregation ensured better treatment for Germans than for many black Americans. The poet Witter Bynner placed one of these incidents to verse:

> On a train in Texas German prisoners eat
>   With white American soldiers, seat by seat,
> While black American soldiers sit apart—
>   The white men eating meat, the black men heart.

No less than black men, black women in the military were also subject to brutality in the Jim Crow South. When they failed to move along fast enough, three black women in the Women's Army Corps (WACs) were brutally assaulted by civilian police in a Kentucky railroad station. When African Americans resisted such treatment, racial violence erupted at Fort Bragg, N.C.; Fort Dix, N.J.; and other military bases.

Racial discrimination in the military was part of a broader pattern of hostility toward blacks in American society. Attracted by new jobs created by the war effort, nearly 1.6 million blacks moved into the nation's cities. The percentage of blacks living in urban areas rose from less than 50 percent in 1940 to nearly 60 percent in 1945. Western cities such as Los Angeles, San Francisco, and Seattle now joined established northern and southern cities as major centers of black urban population growth. Between 1940 and 1945, the black population of Los Angeles County rose from about 75,000 to 150,000. Seattle's black population leaped from 3,800 to nearly 10,000. At the same time, established midwestern and northeastern cities attracted large numbers of new blacks. In the three-year period from 1940 to 1943, Detroit's black population increased by 50,000. As the black urban population increased, race relations deteriorated and violence broke out in several cities. One example was the so-called zoot suit riots, in which white sailors and civilians attacked African-American and Latino residents. Marked by their dress—broad felt hats, pegged trousers, and pocket knives on gold chains—as well as their color, African-American and Latino youth were assaulted in Los Angeles, San Diego, Long Beach, Chicago, Detroit, and Philadelphia.

Racial violence went well beyond the "zoot suit" confrontations. The most serious conflicts occurred in Harlem and Detroit. In 1943 a policeman shot a black soldier and touched off the Harlem riot, which resulted in at least 5 deaths, 500 injuries, hundreds of arrests, and $5 million in property damage. The actor Sidney Poitier later recalled his experience of the riot: "In a restaurant downtown where I was working I heard that there was trouble in Harlem. After work I took a train uptown, came up out of the subway, and there was chaos everywhere—cops, guns, debris and broken glass all over the street. Many stores had been set on fire, and the commercial district on 125th Street looked as if it had been bombed." An investigative reporter for the New York newspaper *PM* also reported on the riot: "Harlem yesterday morning . . . resembled a bombed-out city wherein destruction miraculously stopped

An angry mob of whites chases a black man (indicated by the arrow) through the streets of Detroit during a 1943 race riot that left 23 people dead.

at the first story. Virtually every show window along the main shopping districts was shattered, their contents cleaned out or in disorder."

The confrontation in Detroit left behind even more deaths, injuries, and arrests. On June 20, 1943, more than 100,000 Detroiters crowded the city's Belle Isle Amusement Park to escape the sweltering summer heat. Before long, violence between blacks and whites broke out at the park's casino, ferry dock, playgrounds, and bus stops. The violence soon spilled over into the black Paradise Valley area. At a local club, a patron took the microphone and announced: "There's a riot at Belle Isle! The whites have killed a colored lady and her baby. Thrown them over a bridge. Everybody come on! There's free transportation outside!" Although the report of the death of a black woman and her child was false, by early morning African Americans had smashed windows and

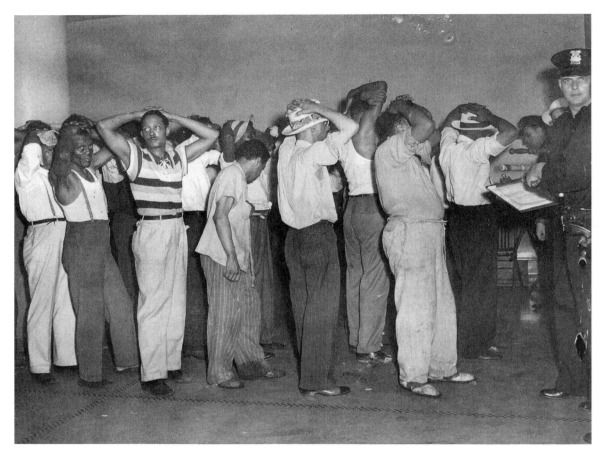

looted numerous white-owned stores on Hastings Avenue. Only the arrival of federal troops put down the violence, which resulted in 34 deaths, 675 injuries, nearly 1,900 arrests, and an estimated $2 million in property damage. In both the Harlem and Detroit riots, most of those killed, injured, or arrested were blacks, while the damaged property belonged almost exclusively to whites.

Racial violence in Detroit and elsewhere was intertwined with the growing residential segregation of African Americans in the cities. As it had during the depression years, federal housing policy reinforced patterns of residential segregation. For example, in 1941 the Federal Public Housing Authority (FPHA) approved the Sojourner Truth Housing Project in Detroit, named for a black abolitionist. Although the project was designated for black occupancy, it was located in a predominantly

The army had to restore order in Detroit after fierce racial violence broke out in 1943. Here, a group of black men waits to be searched for weapons in a police station.

white working-class neighborhood. When local residents protested, federal authorities changed their minds and decided to exclude blacks. The project was then handed over to whites. Only the vigorous protests of the black community, organized by the Sojourner Truth Citizens Committee and supported by the United Auto Workers union, regained for African Americans the right to live in the project.

On the other hand, the federal government soon established an all-white project at the Ford Motor Company's new Willow Run factory. Although blacks and their CIO allies tried to persuade federal officials to permit blacks and whites to occupy the units, the FPHA insisted on a policy of racial segregation. Such housing policies, along with restrictive employment practices and discrimination in the military, embittered black–white relations in the city of Detroit and fueled the underlying forces leading to the 1943 race riot.

African Americans did not passively accept racial discrimination in the defense program. Popularized by the *Pittsburgh Courier*, the militant "Double V" campaign against social injustice at home and abroad enabled African Americans to declare their loyalty to the war effort without abandoning their thrust for equal rights at home. As early as the summer of 1940, the NAACP criticized the navy's policy of recruiting blacks as messmen only. The organization emphasized the injustice of using black tax dollars to finance opportunities for whites while denying such opportunities to blacks.

> Our taxes help to keep up the Naval Academy at Annapolis where our boys may not attend. They help to maintain the numerous naval bases, navy yards, and naval air bases, from which we are excluded. . . . The training in numerous trades and skills which thousands of whites receive and use later in civilian life is not for us. The [health] care . . . the travel and education—all at the expense of the taxpayers—are for whites only. This is the price we pay for being classified as a race, as mess attendants only: At the same time we are supposed to be able to appreciate what our white fellow citizens declare to be the "vast difference" between American Democracy and Hitlerism.

The fight against discrimination in the military was not limited to male branches of the service. Under the leadership of Mabel K. Staupers, executive director of the National Association of Colored Graduate Nurses, African Americans waged a vigorous fight to integrate the Army and Navy Nurse Corps. The army established a quota on the number of black women accepted for service, while the navy barred them altogether. In her campaign to end such discrimination, Staupers tried to enlist the support of white nurses' groups. In a letter to attorney William H. Hastie, a black appointee in the War Department, she explained her position: "Although we know that pressure from Negro groups will mean something, nevertheless, I am spending all of my time contacting white groups, especially nursing groups. I have a feeling that if enough white nursing organizations can register a protest and enough white organizations of influence other than nurses do the same, it will create in the minds of the people in the War Department the feeling that white people do not need protection in order to save themselves from being cared for by Negro personnel." Only an acute shortage of white nurses by early 1945 helped end the army's quota system and break the barriers to black women nurses in the navy.

African Americans also attacked racial discrimination in war industries with government contracts. On its July 1940 cover, the NAACP's *Crisis* featured an airplane factory marked "For Whites Only" with the caption "Warplanes—Negro Americans may not build them, repair them, or fly them, but they must help pay for them." A journalist for the *Pittsburgh Courier* wrote, "Our war is not against Hitler in Europe, but against Hitler in America. Our war is not to defend democracy, but to get a democracy we have never had."

The African-American quest for social justice gained its most potent expression in the emergence of the militant March on Washington Movement (MOWM). Spearheaded by A. Philip Randolph of the Brotherhood of Sleeping Car Porters (BSCP), the MOWM was launched in 1941 following a meeting of civil rights groups in Chicago. The critical moment came when a black woman angrily addressed the chair: "Mr. Chairman . . . we ought to throw 50,000 Negroes around the White House, bring them from all over the country, in jalopies, in trains and any way they can get there, and throw them around the White House and keep them there until we can get some action from the White House." Randolph not only seconded the proposal but offered himself and the BSCP as leaders: "I agree with the sister. I will be very happy to throw [in] my organization's resources and offer myself as a leader of such a movement."

By early June, the MOWM had established march headquarters in Harlem, Brooklyn, Washington, D.C., Pittsburgh, Detroit, Chicago, St. Louis, and San Francisco. The movement spread through the major rail centers and soon joined forces with local NAACP and Urban League

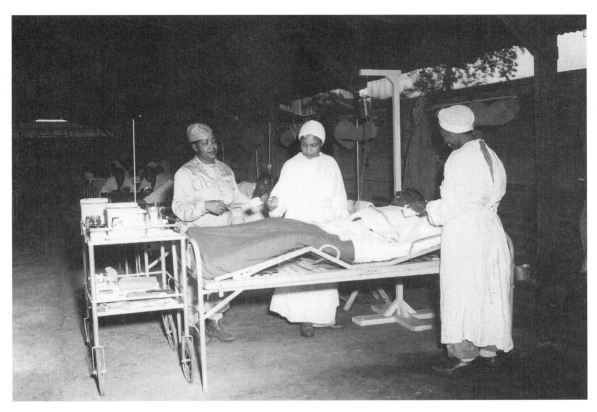

Black nurses tend to a ward full of injured servicemen at a field hospital in New Guinea. A severe shortage of white nurses led the armed forces—reluctantly— to enlist black ones.

chapters, churches, and fraternal orders. The *Black Worker,* the official organ of the BSCP, became the official newspaper of the MOWM. The paper's May issue reprinted the official call to march:

> We call upon you to fight for jobs in National Defense. We call upon you
> to struggle for the integration of Negroes in the armed forces . . . of the
> Nation. . . . We call upon you to demonstrate for the abolition of Jim
> Crowism in all Government departments and defense employment. . . . The
> Federal Government cannot with clear conscience call upon private industry
> and labor unions to abolish discrimination based upon race and color so long
> as it practices discrimination itself against Negro Americans.

The MOWM helped to mobilize the masses of black working people as well as the middle and upper classes. According to Randolph, "It was apparent . . . that some unusual, bold and gigantic effort must be made to awaken the American people and the President of the Nation to the realization that the Negroes were the victims of sharp and unbearable

103

oppression, and that the fires of resentment were flaming higher and higher." Although the MOWM welcomed liberal white support, Randolph insisted that African Americans lead the movement. Randolph was wary of the labor movement, the major political parties, and the growing Communist influence in black organizations like the National Negro Congress (NNC). When the Communist party gained control of the NNC in early 1940, for example, Randolph resigned from the presidency and soon left the organization. Ralph Bunche reported on Randolph's departing speech, which urged blacks to pursue a more independent course in their struggle against racial subordination:

> Randolph's speech was a very fair one. He merely cautioned the Negro that it would be foolish for him to tie up his own interests with the foreign policy of the Soviet Union or any other nation of the world. Nor would the Negro be sensible in hoping that through tying himself to any American organization, political or labor, he would find a ready solution for the problems. He cautioned the Congress against too close a relationship with any organization, mentioning the major parties, the Communist Party, the Socialist Party (of which he is a member) and the CIO. He expressed the view that the Negro Congress should remain independent and non-partisan and that it should be built up by Negro effort alone.

Although Roosevelt resisted the movement as long as he could, the MOWM finally produced results. Roosevelt met with Randolph and Walter White of the NAACP on June 18, 1941. Randolph, Walter White and others later recalled the details of the initial meeting with FDR. The following represents a composite of their reminiscences:

> "Mr. President, time is running on. You are quite busy, I know. But what we want to talk with you about is the problem of jobs for Negroes in defense industries. Our people are being turned away at factory gates because they are colored. They can't live with this thing. Now, what are you going to do about it?"
>
> "Well, Phil, what do you want me to do?"
>
> "Mr. President, we want you to do something that will enable Negro workers to get work in these plants."
>
> "Why," Roosevelt replied, "I surely want them to work, too. I'll call up the heads of the various defense plants and have them see to it that Negroes are given the same opportunity to work in defense plants as any other citizen in the country."
>
> "We want you to do more than that," Randolph said. "We want something concrete, something tangible, definite, positive, and affirmative."
>
> "What do you mean?"

"Mr. President, we want you to issue an executive order making it mandatory that Negroes be permitted to work in these plants."

"Well, Phil," Roosevelt replied, "you know I can't do that. If I issue an executive order for you, then there'll be no end to other groups coming in here and asking me to issue executive orders for them, too. In any event, I couldn't do anything unless you called off this march of yours. Questions like this can't be settled with a sledge hammer."

"I'm sorry, Mr. President, the march cannot be called off."

"How many people do you plan to bring?" Roosevelt wanted to know.

"One hundred thousand, Mr. President."

Roosevelt seemed torn between alarm and disbelief. Perhaps this was a bluff. He turned to Walter White, as if to a man whose word he could trust, looked White squarely in the eye for a few seconds, and asked, "Walter, how many people will really march?"

White's eyes did not blink. He said, "One hundred thousand, Mr. President."

"You can't bring 100,000 Negroes to Washington," Roosevelt said. "Somebody might get killed."

Randolph said that that was unlikely, especially if the President himself came out and addressed the gathering.

Roosevelt was not amused. "Call it off," he said curtly, "and we'll talk again."

Randolph replied, "I shall have to stand by the pledge I've made to the people."

It was Mayor La Guardia [of New York] who broke the impasse. "Gentlemen," he said, "it is clear that Mr. Randolph is not going to call off the march, and I suggest we all begin to seek a formula."

A week later, on June 24, 1941, FDR issued Executive Order 8802, banning racial discrimination in government employment, defense industries, and training programs. Roosevelt also established the Fair Employment Practices Committee (FEPC) to enforce the provisions of the executive order. The FEPC was empowered to receive, investigate, and address complaints of racial discrimination in the defense programs.

Executive Order 8802 proved to be a turning point in African-American history. It linked the struggle of African Americans even more closely to the Democratic party and helped to transform the federal government into a significant ally. African Americans used the FEPC to broaden their participation in the war effort, but this proved to be a slow process. Although an estimated 118,000 blacks were trained for industrial, professional, and clerical jobs in 1941, by the end of 1942 only a

EXECUTIVE ORDER

REAFFIRMING POLICY OF FULL PARTICIPATION IN
THE DEFENSE PROGRAM BY ALL PERSONS, REGARDLESS
OF RACE, CREED, COLOR, OR NATIONAL ORIGIN, AND
DIRECTING CERTAIN ACTION IN FURTHERANCE OF
SAID POLICY.

WHEREAS it is the policy of the United States to encourage
full participation in the national defense program by all
citizens of the United States, regardless of race, creed, color,
or national origin, in the firm belief that the democratic way
of life within the Nation can be defended successfully only with
the help and support of all groups within its borders; and

WHEREAS there is evidence that available and needed workers
have been barred from employment in industries engaged in defense
production solely because of considerations of race, creed, color,
or national origin, to the detriment of workers' morale and of
national unity:

NOW, THEREFORE, by virtue of the authority vested in me by
the Constitution and the statutes, and as a prerequisite to the
successful conduct of our national defense production effort, I
do hereby reaffirm the policy of the United States that there shall
be no discrimination in the employment of workers in defense
industries *or Government* because of race, creed, color, or national origin, and
I do hereby declare that it is the duty of employers and of labor
organizations, in furtherance of said policy and of this order, to
provide for the full and equitable participation of all workers
in defense industries, without discrimination because of race, creed,
color, or national origin;

And it is hereby ordered as follows:

1. All departments and agencies of the Government of the
United States concerned with vocational and training programs for
defense production shall take special measures appropriate to assure
that such programs are administered without discrimination because
of race, creed, color, or national origin;

Faced with the threat of 100,000 blacks marching on Washington, President Roosevelt bowed to pressure from A. Philip Randolph and other black leaders and issued Executive Order 8802, which officially outlawed racial discrimination in defense industries.

- 2 -

2. All contracting agencies of the Government of the United
States shall include in all defense contracts hereafter negotiated
by them a provision obligating the contractor not to discriminate
against any worker because of race, creed, color, or national
origin;

3. There is established in the Office of Production Management a Committee on Fair Employment Practice, which shall consist
of a chairman and four other members to be appointed by the
President. The chairman and members of the Committee shall serve
as such without compensation but shall be entitled to actual and
necessary transportation, subsistence and other expenses incidental
to performance of their duties. The Committee shall receive and
investigate complaints of discrimination in violation of the provisions of this order and shall take appropriate steps to redress
grievances which it finds to be valid. The Committee shall also
recommend to the several departments and agencies of the Government
of the United States and to the President all measures which may be
deemed by it necessary or proper to effectuate the provisions of
this order.

THE WHITE HOUSE,

June   , 1941.

small percentage had obtained employment in defense industries. Industrial firms in the North and South dragged their feet putting fair employment practices into effect. In January 1942, the FEPC cited five Milwaukee firms for racial discrimination against the city's black workers and directed them "to give written notice" that they would end such practices. Shipyard companies in Houston, Galveston, Mobile, New Orleans, and Tampa advertised widely for white women and boys to pursue training as welders, but they resisted the FEPC's push to place black welders. Southern colleges also barred blacks from training programs supported by federal money, forcing African Americans to travel to a limited number of black training centers. In Mobile, when the FEPC pressured the Alabama Drydock and Shipbuilders Company to upgrade some black workers to the job of welder, the company supported the walkout and a riot of some 20,000 white workers, who quit in protest against the employment of black workers.

Southeastern railroads offered even stronger evidence of white resistance. In 1940, with the support of the National Mediation Board, the southeastern railroads and their exclusively white unions signed the notorious "Washington Agreement," designed to eliminate black firemen from employment. Black workers soon challenged the Washington Agreement under the new FEPC guidelines. The FEPC ordered the companies and unions to adjust their policies "so that all needed workers shall be hired and all company employees shall be promoted without regard to race, creed, color or national origin." When the railroads and unions defied the order, African Americans took their case to court, but nothing was done until 1944 when a U.S. Supreme Court ruling, *Bester William Steele* v. *The Louisville and Nashville Company, Brotherhood of Locomotive Firemen and Engineers,* upheld their claims. Every year, at the annual meetings of the AFL, A. Philip Randolph exhorted white workers to end racial bias. He repeatedly stated that "it won't do for the trade union movement, which ought to be the bulwark of democracy and which ought to maintain the tradition of democracy, to say 'no,' you cannot participate in our organization, because you are not competent, because you are not worthwhile, because you are colored, because you are not white."

Despite the persistence of discrimination, as the wartime labor shortages increased, the FEPC played a key role in helping black work-

ers find jobs in defense plants. The number of blacks in war production increased from less than 3 percent in March 1942 to more than 8 percent in 1944. And unlike what had happened during World War I, substantial numbers now moved into semiskilled and skilled positions. As St. Clair Drake and Horace R. Cayton noted in their study of Chicago during the period, "The Second World War broke the ceiling at the level of semi-skilled work and integrated thousands of Negroes as skilled laborers in the electrical and light manufacturing industries, from which they had been barred by custom, and in the vast new airplane-engine factories. . . . They also began to filter into minor managerial and clerical positions in increasing numbers."

While the AFL unions and the railroad brotherhoods did much to hamper this process, the unions of the Congress of Industrial Organiza-tions often supported the FEPC and the claims of black workers and helped them to break the job ceiling. At its annual convention in 1941,

At a parade in Detroit in 1944, the NAACP spon-sored this float, shaped like a Ku Klux Klan costume, to encourage the AFL to end discrimination in its unions.

for example, the CIO denounced racially discriminatory hiring policies as a "direct attack against our nation's policy to build democracy in our fight against Hitlerism." A year later, the organization established its own Committee to Abolish Racial Discrimination and urged its affiliates to support national policy against discrimination: "When a decision to employ minority group workers is made, the union must be prepared to stand behind it." Although black workers faced ongoing obstacles in their struggle for skilled, managerial, and clerical positions, by the end of World War II they claimed the CIO, the Democratic party, and the federal government as important allies in their struggle for social change.

After a long period of unemployment, relief, and public service work, African Americans gained a foothold in the industrial economy during World War II. Although war production created new economic opportunities for African Americans, the path was fraught with numerous difficulties. Labor unions, employers, and the state pursued racially discriminatory employment policies. Only the organizational and political activities of African Americans in their own behalf ensured access to industrial jobs and full employment. They had learned that "closing ranks" in support of the nation did not mean they had to suspend their own struggle for equality. The "Double V" campaign for victory at home and abroad, the March on Washington Movement, and the growing use of the federal government to secure their aims helped to write a new chapter in the history of African Americans and set the stage for the modern civil rights movement of the postwar years.

TOWARD THE MODERN CIVIL RIGHTS MOVEMENT

◇ ◇ ◇

The struggles and successes of African Americans during the Great Depression and World War II established the framework for the development of black life during the postwar years.

After the war, the black middle class would continue to expand and black activism increased to the point that it changed into what we know as the modern civil rights movement. Designed to dismantle the system of racial discrimination and segregation in the North as well as Jim Crow in the South, the civil rights movement was deeply rooted in the continuing transformation of rural blacks into a new urban people. While African Americans would experience significant progress in the postwar years, they would continue to occupy a very unstable position in the urban political economy. Black awareness of class and racial inequality, especially as it existed in the cities, fueled militant demands for social change.

In the years after World War II, African Americans continued their transition from a southern-rural to a nationwide-urban population. The percentage of blacks living in urban areas rose from 62.4 percent in 1950 to more than 80 percent by 1970. At the same time, blacks living in the South dropped from nearly 70 percent of the total African-American population in 1950 to just over 50 percent by the late 1960s. African Americans were now nearly evenly distributed between the North and West on the one hand and the South on the other.

An unemployed man sits on a park bench in Washington, D.C. In the years after World War II the number of blacks moving from rural areas to cities continued to rise.

111

Along with the persistence of racial segregation and discrimination in the rural South, the continuation of New Deal economic programs heightened the movement of blacks off the land. Also, in the South large landowners gained increasing control of southern agriculture and applied new labor-saving technologies.

Tractors, flamethrowers, herbicides, and mechanical cotton pickers helped to undercut the position of black agricultural labor and fueled the movement of blacks into cities. As blacks moved off the land in growing numbers, they were absorbed by the nation's mass production industries—especially the steel, rubber, meatpacking, and automobile sectors. Building upon the gains of the war years, blacks also slowly expanded their numbers in new enterprises, including the aircraft, electronics, and chemical industries.

Workers at a meatpacking plant. During the years after World War II blacks thronged to the nation's mass production industries. At the same time, industrial firms gradually left the inner cities for suburban locations, causing new employment problems for black workers.

Helped by the production demands of the cold war and later the Korean War in 1951, African Americans improved their economic position. The per capita wages and salaries of black men increased from 54 percent of white males in 1947 to 64 percent in 1951. Unemployment among black men and women also reached a postwar low, 4.4 and 3.7 percent, respectively. Moreover, a core of black workers had been employed in urban industries since the 1920s and 1930s and now benefited from seniority rules. Even more remarkably, the employment of black men in their 20s rose to more than 90 percent by 1953. Based upon the expanding economic base provided by black workers in old and new sectors of the nation's economy, the black middle class also expanded during the 1950s. The percentage of black men in middle-class occupations rose from 24 percent in 1950 to 35.3 percent by the late 1960s. At the same time, the number of black women in professional occupations nearly doubled. Black women also gained increasing access to clerical and sales jobs as the percentage of black women in agricultural and domestic service occupations steadily declined.

Although African Americans improved their economic position as a result of the Korean War, they nonetheless faced new problems in the postwar economy. The return of white World War II veterans, coupled with a massive migration of rural southern whites into the nation's urban centers, helped to undercut the potential gains of African Americans. More important, however, the growing transformation of the nation's economy from a goods-producing one to a new service-producing economy heightened the difficulties of black workers. As manufacturers relocated to suburban areas or took up residence in the sunbelt states of the South and Southwest, manufacturing firms in the nation's central cities dropped from about 66 percent of the total in 1947 to about 40 percent by the late 1960s. Although the U.S. Supreme Court ruled restrictive housing covenants unconstitutional in 1948, federal housing policies (particularly those of the Federal Housing Administration and the public housing authorities), exclusionary zoning laws, and discriminatory real estate and lending agencies reinforced residential segregation and separated blacks from jobs in the expanding industrial suburbs.

Following the Korean War, African Americans suffered from rising and disproportionate levels of unemployment. Their unemployment rate rose to nearly twice the rate of whites from the early 1950s through the

1960s. In this same period, the unemployment rate of black youth climbed to nearly three times the rate of their white counterparts. Despite a significant core of blacks with seniority by the early 1950s, African Americans continued to occupy the lower rungs of the industrial ladder, with less seniority than whites. They remained the "last hired and first fired" during the economic downturns and layoffs that came in the wake of plant relocations and the growing use of labor-saving technology. Although black women improved their position during the period, they faced competition from the rising numbers of white women who entered the labor force in the postwar years. While the percentage of black women in the work force remained relatively stable at about 44 percent, the number of white women in the labor force increased from 30 percent in 1948 to nearly 40 percent during the 1960s.

In the postwar years, the alliance between African Americans, the federal government, and the labor movement frayed. The federal government refused to renew the Fair Employment Practices Committee following its expiration in the postwar years, and left blacks vulnerable to the resurgence of racial discrimination in industrial jobs. In 1947, Congress enacted the repressive Taft-Hartley Act (which limited the ability of unions to organize and encouraged the enactment of right-to-work laws in southern states) and launched a vigorous campaign to eliminate Communists from civil rights and labor organizations. Under pressure from the House Un-American Activities Committee (HUAC), the NAACP, the AFL, and the CIO purged Communists from their ranks. The removal of Communists weakened the alliance for social change and set the stage for the merger of the previously radical CIO with its conservative AFL counterpart in 1955.

As the new AFL-CIO got under way, some African Americans hoped that the merger would strengthen the hand of African Americans. Two black labor leaders, A. Philip Randolph and Willard Townsend, received leadership positions in the new union. Although they soon used their positions to publicize the grievances of black workers, their presence did little to relieve the disappointment of black workers. From the outset, the new union admitted the Brotherhood of Locomotive Firemen and the Brotherhood of Railroad Trainmen, which barred blacks from membership by constitutional provisions. Even during the organizing drives of the depression and World War II, the AFL had exhibited little interest in the welfare of black workers. Nevertheless, it received more

Members of the United Packinghouse Workers of America, Local 309, on strike against the W&W Pickle Company in Montgomery, Alabama, December 17, 1951.

than 75 percent of the executive council positions in the new union. When African Americans filed suit against the discriminatory practices of member unions, the new AFL-CIO opposed their claims in court. The black press, the NAACP, and black labor leaders increasingly complained of racial discrimination in the labor movement.

As the AFL-CIO neglected the needs of black workers, African Americans again turned inward, strengthened their connections with each other, and charted an independent course. As early as 1951, black workers formed the National Negro Labor Council (NNLC). Under the leadership of William R. Hood, its first president, the NNLC staged strikes, mobilized boycotts, and organized job training programs to assist in the upgrading of black workers. The organization also demanded black representation in a broad range of leadership positions in the labor movement. Unfortunately, the organization soon declined under the twin

opposition of organized white labor and the HUAC. In 1959, under the leadership of A. Philip Randolph, African Americans formed the American Negro Labor Council and pushed for membership in the predominantly white unions, employment, promotion on the job and access to the union's executive, administrative, and staff positions.

The formation of the American Negro Labor Council was closely intertwined with the development of a new grass roots social movement. Black religious, fraternal, political, and labor organizations had already begun protests and civil disobedience campaigns that would develop into the modern civil rights movement. That movement, which transcended regional, class, and racial boundaries, emphasized nonviolent direct action and transformed the African-American struggle into a national and even international cause.

Beginning with a successful Montgomery, Alabama, bus boycott in 1955, the movement gained its most forceful public expression in the 1963 March on Washington for Jobs and Freedom, where Martin Luther

Led by A. Philip Randolph, Martin Luther King, Jr., and other black leaders, the March on Washington for Jobs and Freedom drew over 200,000 people to the nation's capital in 1963.

King, Jr., delivered his renowned "I Have a Dream" speech. Organized by A. Philip Randolph and black unionists in the American Negro Labor Council, the March on Washington not only symbolized the coming of age of the civil rights movement but accented its deep roots in the struggles of the Great Depression and World War II. A year later, Randolph again told the nation that the black community would carry on the fight for social justice: "We will continue our boycotts, sit-ins, and civil disobedience until grievances are completely redressed. . . . We are in the midst of a full-dress revolution. We demand, we do not beg or plead, fundamental economic changes. Even Jesus Christ participated in civil disobedience. We have no alternative."

Despite their growing political independence in the postwar years, African Americans did not, indeed could not, act entirely alone. Although the federal government and labor unions hampered the fight against class and racial inequality, they remained essential actors in the ongoing struggle for social justice. In 1948, President Harry S. Truman issued an executive order banning discrimination in federal employment. During the Korean War, the federal government ended racial segregation in the military. In a series of rulings and decrees, the U.S. Supreme Court and the Interstate Commerce Commission outlawed racial segregation in all interstate travel. In 1954, the Supreme Court handed down its landmark *Brown* v. *Board of Education* decision, which struck down the 1896 *Plessy* v. *Ferguson* ruling and ordered the desegregation of public schools. The executive council of the AFL-CIO later endorsed the decision and urged President Dwight D. Eisenhower to withhold federal funds from states that resisted the order.

Yet, even though these long-overdue federal actions were helpful, the dismantling of the segregationist system and movement to a more open society that included African Americans as full citizens would come about only because of the actions of blacks on their own behalf. Although much would change in the postwar years, this much remained the same.

CHRONOLOGY

NOVEMBER 1928
President Herbert Hoover elected.

OCTOBER 24, 1929
Stock market crashes; Great Depression begins.

MARCH 1931
Eight of the nine Scottsboro Boys are tried and convicted of rape in an Alabama court.

1931
Communist party assists in the formation of the Alabama Sharecroppers Union.

JANUARY 1932
Hoover administration establishes the Reconstruction Finance Corporation to aid industry.

NOVEMBER 1932
Franklin D. Roosevelt elected President.

1932
U.S. Supreme Court overturns conviction of Scottsboro Boys in *Powell* v. *Alabama* (1932).

1933
New Deal begins.

1933
The National Association for the Advancement of Colored People, the National Urban League, and other civil rights organizations organize the Joint Committee on National Recovery.

1933
Negro History Bulletin begins publication under Carter G. Woodson.

1934
Socialist party organizes the Southern Tenant Farmers Union.

1935
In *Pearson* v. *Murray,* the Maryland Court of Appeals orders the University of Maryland to admit African Americans to the state's all-white law school or to set up a separate law school for blacks; the University of Maryland chooses to admit its first African-American students.

1935
Brotherhood of Sleeping Car Porters and Maids receives an international charter from the American Federation of Labor.

1935
Race riot breaks out in Harlem.

1935
National Labor Relations Act (Wagner Act) is passed by Congress; National Labor Relations Board established.

1935
U.S. Supreme Court again overturns convictions of Scottsboro Boys, in *Norris* v. *Alabama* (1935).

1936
Nearly 600 black organizations form the National Negro Congress; A. Philip Randolph elected its first president.

1937
Brotherhood of Sleeping Car Porters and Maids signs its first contract with the Pullman Company.

1938
Joe Louis defeats German boxer Max Schmeling.

1940
Richard Wright's novel *Native Son* published.

JUNE 1941
A. Philip Randolph organizes March on Washington.

JUNE 24, 1941
FDR issues Executive Order 8802, establishing the Fair Employment Practices Committee.

DECEMBER 7, 1941
Japan attacks Pearl Harbor; United States enters World War II the next day.

1943
Race riots break out in Harlem and Detroit.

1944
Swedish economist Gunnar Myrdal publishes *An American Dilemma: The Negro Problem and Modern Democracy.*

1941–45
Nearly 1 million African Americans serve in the U.S. armed forces during World War II.

FURTHER READING

◇ ◇ ◇

A NOTE ON SOURCES

In the interest of readability, the volumes in this series include no discussion of historiography and no footnotes. As works of synthesis and overview, however, they are greatly indebted to the research and writing of other historians. The principal works drawn on in this volume are among the books listed below.

GENERAL HISTORY OF AFRICAN AMERICANS

Bennett, Lerone, Jr. *Before the Mayflower: A History of Black America.* 6th rev. ed. New York: Viking Penguin, 1988.

———. *The Shaping of Black America.* New York: Viking Penguin, 1993.

Franklin, John Hope, and August Meier. *Black Leaders of the 20th Century.* Urbana: University of Illinois Press, 1982.

Franklin, John Hope, and Alfred A. Moss, Jr. *From Slavery to Freedom: A History of Negro Americans.* 6th ed. New York: Knopf, 1988.

Gates, Henry L., Jr. *A Chronology of African-American History from 1445–1980.* New York: Amistad, 1980.

Harding, Vincent. *There Is a River: The Black Struggle for Freedom in America.* San Diego: Harcourt Brace, 1981.

Meltzer, Milton. *The Black Americans: A History in Their Own Words.* Rev. ed. New York: HarperCollins, 1984.

Quarles, Benjamin. *The Negro in the Making of America.* 3rd ed. New York: Macmillan, 1987.

THE DEPRESSION AND WORLD WAR II

Kusmer, Kenneth L., ed. *Depression, War, and the New Migration, 1930–1960.* Vol. 6 of *Black Communities and Urban Development in America, 1720–1960.* New York: Garland, 1991.

McElvaine, Robert S. *The Great Depression: America, 1929-1941.* New York: Times Books, 1984.

Nash, Gerald D. *The Crucial Era: The Great Depression and World War II, 1929–1945.* 2nd ed. New York: St. Martin's, 1992.

Sitkoff, Harvard. *A New Deal for Blacks: The Emergence of Civil Rights as a National Issue: The Depression Decade.* New York: Oxford University Press, 1978.

Sternsher, Bernard, ed. *The Negro in Depression and War: Prelude to Revolution, 1930–1945.* Chicago: Quadrangle, 1969.

Wright, Richard, and Edwin Rosskam. *12 Million Black Voices.* New York: Thunder's Mouth, 1941.

AFRICAN-AMERICAN CULTURE AND INSTITUTIONS

Frankl, Ron. *Duke Ellington.* New York: Chelsea House, 1988.

Frazier, E. Franklin, and C. Eric Lincoln. *The Negro Church in America and the Black Church Since Frazier.* New York: Schocken, 1974.

Hazard-Gordon, Katrina. *Jookin': The Rise of Social Dance Formations in African-American Culture.* Philadelphia: Temple University Press, 1990.

Jakoubek, Robert. *Joe Louis.* New York: Chelsea House, 1989.

Jones, LeRoi (Amiri Baraka). *Blues People: The Negro Experience in White America and the Music That Developed from It.* New York: William Morrow, 1963.

Levine, Lawrence. *Black Culture and Black Consciousness: Afro-American Folk Thought from Slavery to Freedom*. New York: Oxford University Press, 1977.

Southern, Eileen. *The Music of Black Americans: A History*. New York: Norton, 1971.

Urban, Joan. *Richard Wright*. New York: Chelsea House, 1989.

BLACK COMMUNITY STUDIES

Broussard, Albert S. *Black San Francisco: The Struggle for Racial Equality in the West, 1900–1954*. Lawrence: University Press of Kansas, 1993.

Daniels, Douglas Henry. *Pioneer Urbanites: A Social and Cultural History of Black San Francisco*. Philadelphia: Temple University Press, 1980.

Drake, St. Clair, and Horace R. Cayton. *Black Metropolis: A Study of Negro Life in a Northern City*. 2 vols. 1944. Reprint, New York: Harcourt, Brace and World, 1962.

Greenberg, Cheryl Lynn. *Or Does It Explode? Black Harlem in the Great Depression*. New York: Oxford University Press, 1991.

Lewis, Earl. *In Their Own Interests: Race, Class and Power in Twentieth Century Norfolk*. Berkeley: University of California Press, 1991.

Taylor, Quintard. *The Forging of a Black Community: Seattle's Central District from 1870 through the Civil Rights Era*. Seattle: University of Washington Press, 1994.

Trotter, Joe William, Jr. *Black Milwaukee: The Making of an Industrial Proletariat, 1915–45*. Urbana: University of Illinois Press, 1985.

POLITICS, LEADERSHIP, AND RACE RELATIONS

Anderson, Jervis. *A. Philip Randolph: A Biographical Portrait*. Berkeley: University of California Press, 1986.

Grant, Nancy L. *TVA and Black Americans: Planning for the Status Quo*. Philadelphia: Temple University Press, 1990.

Kelley, Robin D. G. *Hammer and Hoe: Alabama Communists during the Great Depression*. Chapel Hill: University of North Carolina Press, 1990.

Kirby, John B. *Black Americans in the Roosevelt Era: Liberalism and Race*. Knoxville: University of Tennessee Press, 1992.

Mintz, Sidney W., and Richard Price. *The Birth of African-American Culture: An Anthropological Perspective*. Boston: Beacon Press, 1992.

Myrdal, Gunnar. *An American Dilemma: The Negro Problem and Modern Democracy*. 2 vols. 1944. Reprint, New York: Pantheon, 1962.

Naison, Mark. *Communists in Harlem During the Depression*. Urbana: University of Illinois Press, 1983.

Nieman, Donald G. *Promises to Keep: African-Americans and the Constitutional Order, 1776 to the Present*. New York: Oxford University Press, 1991.

Shapiro, Herbert. *White Violence and Black Response: From Reconstruction to Montgomery*. Amherst: University of Massachusetts Press, 1988.

Urquhart, Brian. *Ralph Bunche*. New York: Norton, 1993.

Wolters, Raymond. *Negroes and the Great Depression: The Problem of Economic Recovery*. Westport, Conn.: Greenwood, 1970.

WORK AND LABOR RELATIONS

Dickerson, Dennis C. *Out of the Crucible: Black Steelworkers in Western Pennsylvania, 1875–1980*. Albany: State University of New York Press, 1986.

Foner, Philip S. *Organized Labor and the Black Workers, 1619–1973*. New York: International Publishers, 1974.

Hanley, Sally. *A. Philip Randolph*. New York: Chelsea House, 1989.

Harris, William H. *Keeping the Faith: A. Philip Randolph, Milton P. Webster, and the Brotherhood of Sleeping Car Porters, 1925–37*. Urbana: University of Illinois Press, 1977.

———. *The Harder We Run: Black Workers Since the Civil War*. New York: Oxford University Press, 1982.

Meier, August, and Elliott Rudwick. *Black Detroit and the Rise of the UAW*. New York: Oxford University Press, 1979.

Painter, Nell Irvin. *The Narrative of Hosea Hudson: His Life as a Communist*. Cambridge: Harvard University Press, 1979.

Rosengarten, Theodore. *All God's Dangers: The Life of Nate Shaw*. New York: Avon, 1974.

Trotter, Joe William, Jr. *Coal, Class, and Color: Blacks in Southern West Virginia, 1915–32*. Urbana: University of Illinois Press, 1990.

AFRICAN-AMERICAN WOMEN

Giddings, Paula. *When and Where I Enter: The Impact of Black Women on Race and Sex in America*. New York: Bantam, 1984.

Gray, Brenda Clegg. *Black Female Domestics during the Depression in New York City, 1930–1940*. New York: Garland, 1993.

Halasa, Malu. *Mary McLeod Bethune*. New York: Chelsea House, 1989.

Hawks, Joanne V., and Sheila L. Skemp, eds. *Sex, Race, and the Role of Women in the South*. Jackson: University Press of Mississippi, 1983.

Hine, Darlene Clark, et al., eds. *Black Women in America*. Brooklyn, N.Y.: Carlson, 1993.

Hine, Darlene Clark. *Black Women in White: Racial Conflict and Cooperation in the Nursing Profession, 1890–1950*. Bloomington: Indiana University Press, 1989.

Jones, Jacqueline. *Labor of Love, Labor of Sorrow: Black Women, Work and the Family, From Slavery to the Present*. New York: Vintage, 1985.

Lerner, Gerda, ed. *Black Women in White America: A Documentary History*. New York: Vintage, 1973.

INDEX

◇ ◇ ◇

Acknowledgments

◇ ◇ ◇

I wish to thank general editors Earl Lewis and Robin Kelley, and Nancy Toff, Editorial Director for Children's and Young Adult Books at Oxford University Press, for the opportunity to write this book. This series reflects a firm conviction that history and historical scholarship must be made available to all ages. I also wish to acknowledge with appreciation a number of people who provided editorial, clerical, and research assistance. At Oxford University Press, Paul McCarthy, project editor, receives special thanks for his careful editorial work and his selection of appropriate illustrations to accompany the text. In the department of history at Carnegie-Mellon University, I received indispensable clerical and research assistance from Lori Cole, Beverly Goines, Sharon Metcalf, and Kate Aberger. To these able young scholars, I am deeply grateful.

Finally, as always, my work is inspired by my mother, the late Thelma O. Trotter, my wife LaRue, and my thirteen sisters and brothers. Over the years, my nieces and nephews have also become new sources of energy, knowledge, and inspiration. This book is dedicated to them with love. It is also dedicated to young African Americans throughout the diaspora. It is my hope that young people will read these pages and realize that the acquisition of historical knowledge is not only an intellectual challenge but a source of inspiration and empowerment as well.

PICTURE CREDITS

◇ ◇ ◇

JOE WILLIAM TROTTER, JR.

◇ ◇ ◇

Joe William Trotter, Jr., is professor of history at Carnegie-Mellon University. He holds a Ph.D. from the University of Minnesota. Professor Trotter is the author of *Coal, Class, and Color: Blacks in Southern West Virginia, 1915–1932, Black Milwaukee: The Making of an Industrial Proletariat, 1915–1945,* and editor of *The Great Migration in Historical Perspective: New Dimensions of Race, Class, and Gender.* His essays have also appeared in a variety of edited volumes, encyclopedias, and journals, including the *Journal of Urban History, Labor History,* the OAH *Magazine of History,* and the *Encyclopedia of Social History.*

ROBIN D.G. KELLEY

◇ ◇ ◇

Robin D. G. Kelley is professor of history and Africana studies at New York University. He previously taught history and African-American studies at the University of Michigan. He is the author of *Hammer and Hoe: Alabama Communists during the Great Depression,* which received the Eliot Rudwick Prize of the Organization of American Historians and was named Outstanding Book on Human Rights by the Gustavus Myers Center for the Study of Human Rights in the United States. Professor Kelley is also the author of *Race Rebels: Culture, Politics, and the Black Working Class* and co-editor of *Imagining Home: Class, Culture, and Nationalism in the African Diaspora.*

EARL LEWIS

◇ ◇ ◇

Earl Lewis is professor of history and Afroamerican studies at the University of Michigan. He served as director of the university's Center for Afroamerican and African Studies from 1990 to 1993. Professor Lewis is the author of *In Their Own Interests: Race, Class and Power in Twentieth Century Norfolk* and co-author of *Blacks in the Industrial Age: A Documentary History.*